Relatively speaking: developments in research and practice in kinship care

by Paul Nixon

research in practice

www.rip.org.uk

Every Partner in the **research** in **practice** network receives a bulk allocation of free copies of this research review at the time of publication. Additional copies may be purchased at half price. See page 117 for purchasing information. The full text is also available to Partners on our website – **www.rip.org.uk**

Published 2007
ISBN 978-1-904984-19-1

© **research** in **practice**

Other titles in the series:

10 *Disengagement and re-engagement of young people in learning at key stage 3*
   Marian Morris and Charlynne Pullen, 2007

9 *Conduct Disorder in Older Children and Young people:*
   Research messages for practice problems
   Carol Joughin and Dinah Morley, 2007

8 *Professionalism, Partnership and Joined-up Thinking:*
   A research review of front-line working with children and families
   Nick Frost, 2005

7 *Parental mental health problems: messages from research, policy and practice*
   Jo Tunnard, 2004

6 *Disabled parents: examining research assumptions*
   Richard Olsen and Michele Wates, 2003

5 *Parental drug misuse: a review of impact and intervention studies*
   Jo Tunnard, 2002

4 *Parental problem drinking and its impact on children*
   Jo Tunnard, 2002

3 *Commissioning and managing external research:*
   a guide for child care agencies
   Jo Tunnard, 2001

2 *Children and Domestic Violence: a research overview of the impact on children*
   Catherine Humphreys and Audrey Mullender, 2000

1 *The Education of Children in Need: a research overview*
   Ruth Sinclair, 1998

research in practice is a department at Dartington; an international centre for the generation and application of new ideas in the arts, ecology and social justice.

about this research review

research in **practice** aims to make it easier for those who deliver services to children and families – whether they work in local authorities, voluntary organisations, health settings, national government organisations or any of their local partner agencies - to access reliable research, distilled and translated with their particular needs in mind. This series of research reviews covers key practice areas identified by practitioners, and key research strategy issues identified by planners and policy makers. The work and methods of **research in practice** support the promotion of better outcomes for children and families through more effective, multi-professional and multi-agency collaborations, in part by creating and using reliable research evidence.

This review addresses a central challenge for those who increasingly want and must provide personalised services for highly individual problems – most especially around ensuring that children who cannot live with their parents and siblings get the very best placement that our modern and sophisticated society can provide. Placement patterns have changed significantly over the last few decades, from a situation where the majority of children lived in residential care, through the last 15 years or so when foster care became the placement of choice for most children and young people, to the last few years where our refreshed understandings of community have helped us appreciate the wealth of talent, commitment and resource that is on offer from the extended families of those we seek to help. Kinship care is fast becoming a placement of choice, and research is showing just how much it contributes to stability and the maintenance and sometimes healing of family relationships.

This review will be of real value to those who have already been making good use of what families can offer, and of equal value to those who want to build practice with the support of new legislation (due in 2008) to promote better use, support for, and resourcing of these placements. This review will help ensure that local policy and practice is founded on the very best available research evidence, and that this evidence base is added to by their own local evaluations.

Celia Atherton
Director of **research** in **practice**

QUALITY MARK This review has been peer-reviewed by a range of academics based in universities and service agencies, and by practitioners and others seeking to assist the development of evidence-informed practice. We are grateful for the generosity and wisdom of: Gale Burford, Margaret Casey, Elizabeth Cooke, Colleen Eccles, Collette Elliott, Elaine Farmer, Ronny Flynn, Margaret Greenfield, Julia Hennessy, Joan Hunt, Bill Joyce, Lisa Keay, Sal Lodge, Terry Philpott, Chris Rainey, John Randall, Andy Riley, Rosie Smith, Martin Stevens and Robert Tapsfield.

The author would like to thank to give special thanks to Joan Hunt from Oxford University and Robert Tapsfield from Fostering Network for their guidance and advice; Andy Couldrick for his support, Alison Roe for helping gather the research, Kirsten Dixon for checking drafts and references and Mike Doolan and Gale Burford for their mentoring and inspiration.

This work is dedicated to Howard and Mary and Diane and Neville our children's grandparents.

For Nici, Carys, Haydn and Rhianna

about referencing

References are grouped at the back of the review according to the nature of the source material, as well as in a more traditional alphabetical listing by author. They are classified into the following categories:

A   UK publications based on primary research on kinship care

B   US publications based on primary research on kinship care

C   Other publications from abroad (outside UK and US) based on primary research on kinship care

D   UK publications based on secondary research, including research and literature reviews

E   UK related primary research on children and their families, social work and foster care

F   Publications based on secondary research from US and other countries

G   General political, theoretical work and training materials

H   Government law, policy documents and guidance

Citations in the text follow the same simple principles. **research** in **practice** has adopted this method as a quick way for readers to identify the type of evidence and to find references with minimal disruption to the flow of the text.

contents

introduction

Kinship care – also known as relative care, network care, kin care, and often called family and friends care in the UK – is attracting increasing international interest. This common child-rearing practice exists in families and communities throughout the world, but there is now a distinct re-emergence of professional and political interest in this type of care for children who cannot live with their parents. Indeed the government's new White Paper *Care Matters: Time for Change* (H7) proposes a major place for the renewed use of kinship care.

The commonly used terms 'kinship care' and 'family and friends care' seem inadequate or too imprecise to describe the wide and varied nature of this type of care arrangement. Perhaps one of the challenges for readers when considering research and practice in this area, is to review what might be the most suitable or usable term. In this review I shall use kinship care, relative care, family and friends care and kin care interchangeably (to avoid tedious repetition), but they shall refer to the same thing. Kinship care is the term used most frequently in the research.

This review examines some of the contemporary issues and trends that come from the current body of knowledge about kinship care. While our understanding about kin care is still in its early stage of development, there do seem to be some distinct themes and lessons emerging from research.

There is wide variation in kinship care arrangements, ranging from those placements privately organised between family or friends, to those formally assessed and controlled by the state. The focus of this paper largely concerns those arrangements for children that are made or supported by the state, where Children's Service Authorities are involved in the lives of families.

A key message within this review is that kinship care appears to offer a good placement choice for many children, but places significant burdens on carers. Furthermore, existing service systems appear to discriminate negatively against this type of placement. By implication, we may need to re-think how we best organise practice and services for kinship care. In particular we may wish to re-conceptualise kinship care as a distinct care type, separate from and different to traditional models of foster care. Kinship care could command its own body of knowledge and evidence base. It may require a distinct policy and service framework that delivers unique financial and support arrangements. And it may suggest a different type of social work assessment and practice tailored for kin care.

In this review, the evidence from UK and abroad will be examined and the impact of kinship care on children, carers and their families will be considered. How current services are responding to the needs of these placements will be critically reviewed. The final section will provide an outline framework for services to kin care and suggest some areas for future development and research. The overall aim is to make a connection between research and practice and ask how we might use kinship care to improve services for children.

why this review?

- State-supported kinship care is increasing significantly in the Western world; we need to understand it better.
- There is renewed government interest in this type of care.
- Research needs to influence services and practice more directly.
- There are enormous regional, national and international variations in the use of kinship care that cannot be accounted for solely by demography.
- Very little information or guidance on kin care is available to professionals compared to that available for foster care, adoption, residential care, etc.
- Services and practices vary significantly – kinship care could be understood as a distinct care type with its own body of knowledge, research, practice, skills and support arrangements.

Flynn (D8) describes kinship care historically as 'under-valued, under-researched, and under-resourced'. The Department for Children, Schools and Families (previously the Department for Education and Skills) has taken a new interest in this area and some significant and radical proposals are contained within the government's new 2007 White Paper *Care Matters: Time for Change* (H7).

The White Paper proposes a new framework for family and friends care and a focus on three types of placement:

a placements with relatives or family friends where a child would otherwise be looked after

b those who are already looked after

c those who are returning from a care placement to be cared for by relatives or friends.

It makes clear the importance of ensuring these placements receive proper recognition and support, and proposes that this will be provided through a new service framework. The government is also proposing a requirement that relatives and friends are properly considered in all child-care cases at the onset of care proceedings.

In the White Paper the government identifies four main concerns that it intends to address:

- national variations in the extent to which family and friends placements are used
- inconsistent application of policy or sheer absence of policy in this area
- lack of transparency of entitlements and services available
- the need for a suitable and consistent approval process for these placements.

(H7)

Many local authority children's services departments are now re-examining their kin care arrangements and managers and practitioners are considering how best to work with these placements.

A burgeoning interest in kinship care developed prior to the publication of *Care Matters* – in part as a response to concerns about the increasing numbers of children having to be cared for away from their birth parents. The Children Act 1989 (H1) had clear aspirations for children to grow up in their families wherever possible, but to date there has been a remarkable lack of policy and service development in this area. Far greater attention has been paid to foster care, residential care, adoption and child protection systems. Kinship care has suffered from a dearth of information and resources. Indeed, policy in this area has been 'almost invisible' (D2) and kinship care has been a low priority.

In the UK, a number of campaign groups and organisations representing carers have fuelled the debate. Fostering Network (previously National Foster Care Association) produced training and resource materials for relative caregivers and social workers (G9). The Grandparents Federation, Grandparents Plus and Family Rights Group have all championed the needs of kinship carers. However, this type of care still appears to be the 'poor relative' compared to other forms of alternative care for children.

The use of kinship care varies dramatically within the Western world and there appears to be a significantly lower percentage use of supported kinship care in the UK, when compared to some other countries (see below). Moreover the use of this placement type also varies enormously within the UK (A19). There are notable variations in practice in the way children and carers are identified, assessed, supported and financially assisted by local authorities (D21, A6, A22).

Historically, the importance of kin networks in the UK appears to have been frequently overlooked by social workers and state agencies. In a review of foster care Berridge (D1) found fostering with relatives was not common practice and suggested that placement with kin may be underused given the evidence of its value. He concluded:

> ...this is particularly curious given that research has consistently found very positive outcomes for children fostered with relatives.
> D1

The principles of the Children Act 1989 (H1), and specific legal duties within it, require the placement of children with relatives or friends (section 23 (6)) when they cannot live with parents, but the numbers of children being placed in such arrangements appears to be relatively low in the UK (see below) (F6). We know less about the number of children being supported outside the public care system although local studies suggest numbers may be significant (A27, D20, A20).

Government assessment of local authorities' performance – notably the Quality Protects, Choice Protects and now the Joint Area Review inspection process – place emphasis on safe and stable placements for children and promote children's access to a range of placement choices. O'Brien (G12) argues that a lack of culturally sensitive services for black families has also spurred interest in kin care. Local authorities must promote a child's sense of identity, respect their cultural heritage and maintain family connections wherever possible.

Interest in kin care has focused the debate on how these placements are best identified, assessed, monitored and supported. However, practitioners and managers are still uncertain operating in this field where policy and guidance is minimal and theory, practice and research knowledge is limited. Policy makers have appeared to struggle and have perhaps avoided providing strong leadership in this area. This may be because there is still no consensus on the extent to which the state should support or monitor relatives who look after children from within their own family network. It may also be that there are concerns about the level of resources needed to support these children and carers properly.

what is kinship care?

There is no single agreed definition of kinship care (just as there is no agreement on what it should be called). Kinship care can describe a range of placement types with extended family, relatives or friends. For some groups, it refers exclusively to extended family and blood-ties; for others, it can include a wider group of non-relative friends, who have also been called 'fictive kin' (F34).

There are definitional differences that will be shaped by the way these placements are identified, sanctioned and supported. These can include, among other arrangements, the private or informal care that families organise themselves, different forms of shared care, children living under residence or special guardianship orders (where the state may or may not have been involved), through to variations of state sanctioned and supported or approved kinship foster care or legally permanent orders including adoption. Indeed, informal kinship care (ie, without the involvement of state agencies) existed before formal arrangements and in many ways underpinned the modern welfare state in the care of children (A28).

Kinship care refers to the care arrangements for a child who cannot live with his or her parents and who is cared for by a family member or family friend with whom the child has some form of relationship or connection. While not providing an explicit and inclusive definition, the Children Act (England and Wales) 1989 appears to encourage broad thinking in this area to include extended family, relative or friend, or 'any person connected with him [the child]' (section 23 (6)). The guidance accompanying the Social Work (Scotland) Act 1995 and the Children (Northern Ireland) Order 1995 both state that local authorities should first explore placements with family and friends before care with non-kin foster carers. But despite these legal requirements, Morgan (A17) surveyed 55 English local authorities and found that only 38 per cent said they had a clear working definition of family and friends care; 62 per cent did not.

Non-legal definitions have paid closer attention to the child's emotional attachment to the carer(s).

> Any living arrangement in which a relative or someone else emotionally close to the child (eg, friends, neighbours, godparents) take primary responsibility for rearing that child.
> F30

In New Zealand kin care is legally inclusive of a wide family group and states the importance of the child's psychological attachment to carers. The family group can include anyone to 'whom the child has a significant psychological attachment' (F6).

A key distinction, then, is made between informal kinship care – a family arrangement taking place outside the child welfare system – and formal kinship care – a placement arranged, supported or approved by state social services (F34). In the USA, state agencies have now adopted this distinction (F44). However, these definitions may oversimplify the more complex nature of what is really happening in practice. Connolly argues:

> ...these terms have been criticised in the literature as being potentially misleading, inaccurate and/or simplistic since situations of care may have both formal and informal elements.
> F6

There are huge variations in definitions of kinship care. In the USA, where to date most of the research on kin care has been conducted, approximately 50 per cent of states define kin only by blood relation, marriage or adoption. Others go further to include family friends, neighbours and godparents, while other states have no formal definition at all (F30).

Where a friend or relative who is not closely related to the child – ie, not a grandparent, uncle, aunt, sibling or step-parent – takes on the caring responsibility for the child at the request of a parent for more than 28 days, then this is legally a private fostering arrangement. Private fostering appears to have been widely neglected (D12, A20) until recently, but it has now become subject to new laws and regulation following the death of Victoria Climbié (E23). Private fostering could be seen as one type of kinship care. The Children Act 2004 (section 44), (H2) and the Children (Private Arrangements for Fostering) Regulations 2005 (H3) strengthened and enhanced the existing arrangements, in part by raising awareness and introducing additional safeguards for children privately fostered. Local authorities have a duty to check on and promote the child's welfare in this context.

Given the wide variations in definition and groups of children that may or may not be included, it is difficult either to compare or generalise findings from research from different locations, because the research may not be referring to the same type of care. However, for the purposes of this review the kinship placements being broadly reviewed here are:

> The care arrangements for a child who cannot live with parents, who is living with a family member or friend, and whose placement has been made or supported by a Children's Services Authority.

For the present, it is likely that kinship care will continue to be defined by its local context and the cultural, historical, legal, procedural, religious or political forces that determine the way people think about families, child rearing praxis and, critically, its relationship to the state.

how prevalent is kinship care?

The number of children living with relatives or friends is difficult to estimate. The lack of an agreed definition, both nationally and internationally, means it is hard to make sense of statistics other than locally. For example, Broad (D2) argues that placements can be classified as 'kinship fostering' without being formally approved as foster care or subject to a fostering agreement.

National statistics appear somewhat variable depending on definitions applied. Between 1996 and 2000 there was a 32 per cent increase in kinship foster care in England, compared to a 15 per cent increase in stranger foster care. Latest validated statistics, based on children looked after at 31 March 2006, show that 12 per cent of children in care (7,300 of 60,300 looked after children) are in kinship foster care (H6). In Scotland 1,600 children are in kinship foster care (A26). However, many of the children in kinship care may not be formally known to children's services. Richards and Tapsfield (D15), extrapolating from the British Attitudes Surveys of 1998 and 2001, suggest that the figure may be as high as 300,000. These figures may be affected by local authorities encouraging carers to apply for residence or special guardianship orders, which would offer the child a legally permanent placement but kin carers may not get the same level of support as foster carers (A22). It is estimated that 200,000 grandparents have grandchildren living with them (D5).

In relation to private fostering, 980 children were reported to be accommodated in these arrangements in England at 31 March 2006, compared with 730 in March 2005 (H6). Again there are no accurate statistics because of the hidden number of children living in private foster care; in 1991 the Department of Health judged there were approximately 2,000 such arrangements (D6), while Philpot (A20) estimated the number could be between 10,000 and 20,000 children living in private foster care.

In many parts of the world care with relatives is still customary. In an overview of international differences, George and van Oudenhoven (F15) reported that in Israel kin care is commonly used. In Surinam it is accepted that children are placed with extended family; raising children is a responsibility that is shared with brothers, sisters and grandparents. Filipinos have always had a tradition of looking after children who cannot live with parents. In Botswana many women who work in urban areas arrange to leave their children in their natal villages, and South Africa has seen large numbers of kin-care arrangements as children are orphaned by the impact of AIDS. Indian families traditionally offer networks of support to the young and vulnerable.

The use of formal relative placements (ie, mandated by children's services) is used extensively in a number of European countries – for example, the Netherlands (C8) and Sweden (C1). Poland gives extended family formal and legal charge of children whose parents cannot look after them; 91 per cent of foster carers are related to the children they care for and 79 per cent of these are grandparents (C13).

The UK appears to support fewer kinship care placements when comparisons are drawn with some other Western countries (see Figure 1). Australia has more than twice the amount of formal kin care, and New Zealand and the USA have three to four times more formal kinship placements than the UK (F6).

New Zealand has seen a fairly rapid increase in the use of formal kin care since the early 1990s, so that it now accounts for 32 per cent of all care placements; half the increase relates to Maori children (C12). Australia makes less use of such arrangements, with kinship care making up 24 per cent of all care placements (F6). Data from 46 US states found kinship care accounted for 35 per cent as a weighted national average of all children in state custody (B47).

Although there are clear cultural and contextual differences with the UK, and while care must be taken in drawing any direct comparisons, it is still worth taking a closer look at the US as one of the most prolific users of formalised kin foster care. In the last 20 years, rising numbers of children have been moving to kinship care in the US, which has seen children increasingly entering the child welfare system due to parental abuse, neglect, drug and alcohol misuse. As in the UK, there has been an increasing demand for foster care that the existing number of non-kin foster placements is struggling to meet. The demand for placements has been compounded by increasing numbers of parents with HIV infection and AIDS which, over time, has led to a greater need for alternative child-care placements (F44).

Figure 1

International comparison of percentage of kinship foster placements used

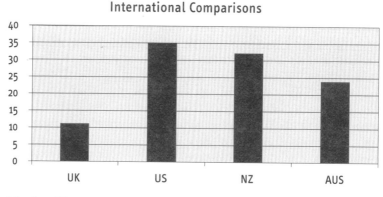

International Comparisons

taken from F6

Statistics show that between 30 and 50 per cent of fostered children in the US are placed in relative homes (B38). Data from 39 states found kin care accounted for 37 per cent of placed children in family foster care (F30). Urban areas have seen the most dramatic increase in these placements. In New York, kinship placements increased from 151 in 1985 to 14,000 in 1989 (F42).

It is estimated that 1.8 million children in the US are in informal, daily, live-in care provided by relatives, with neither parent present in the house. Most of these arrangements are outside any involvement of child welfare services (B23). This figure accounts for 2.2 per cent of the total child population in the US, dwarfing the numbers of children in formalised kinship foster placements (B35). A smaller yet substantial number – 500,000 – are placed with relatives through involvement of child welfare agencies (B46).

There are great variations within and between US states in the use of and support for kin care. Mayfield et al (B47) found the percentage of kin care placements ranging from under 5 per cent in some states to over 50 per cent in others; in some areas it is as high as 60 per cent (G3).

A profile of these carers in the US reveals that they are predominately grandparents on the maternal side of the family (this mirrors the UK – see A22) and that African-Americans have the highest rates of kin placements (F48). Hegar (F20) found that African-American children make up 44 per cent of those living with grandparents without a parent in the home. Ideas about family and cultural patterns are a heavy influence. Kinship care is six times more common for African-American families, and one and half times more common for Hispanic families, than for white non-Hispanic children.

how this review was conducted

The aim of this review was to draw out some of the key themes and patterns in the research to help guide practitioners and managers in thinking about services for kinship care.

The review looked at a range of studies from both the UK and abroad but the list of studies included here is not exhaustive. Much of the research comes from the US and care must be taken when trying to generalise or apply these lessons to a UK context. In reviewing the evidence, I have attempted to separate evidence from the UK, US and other countries.

Studies were drawn from a variety of different sources including published research reports, literature reviews, World Wide Web internet-based information and related research studies that are relevant more generally to the subject of this review.

The quality of research available varies greatly. Some of the studies included here have very small sample sizes and the reader must be cautious about generalising these findings to other situations. The findings from research will be affected by sample size, methodology, location, date, scope and focus of the study, and so on. I have tried in the body of the text to describe briefly the scale and type of the main studies used, so that the reader can draw their own conclusion on the applicability of the findings. Some of the research studies are now quite old and the circumstances on which they report – for example, the nature of social work or the profile of children coming into care – may have changed significantly since they were published. Because there have been so few UK studies on kinship care it was necessary to draw on older studies; however, some of the research here is very current.

In general, many of the earlier studies on kinship care set out to find out about foster care more broadly, and in the process messages about kinship foster care emerged. More recent studies have set out exclusively to find out about kinship care, or to compare kinship care directly with non-kin foster care.

While the core of this review is built around research on kinship care, I have included some related studies. These are taken from relevant primary or secondary research pertinent to the subject matter. There are messages drawn from a wider range of studies in child welfare and foster care, specific to a UK context and legal structure, that may help the reader make sense of the context in which kinship care is occurring. Furthermore, there are some messages about practice in this context, which may be equally applicable.

Messages about social work and social policy are taken into account because an analysis of kinship care cannot not take place in a vacuum. Some attention is paid to wider research into family life and the impact of poverty on older people and children because these are recurring themes in specific studies on kinship care, as are messages about children in public care and social work services to them.

The sources of information for this review were drawn from:

1 Published reports based on primary research on kinship care from the UK, US and other countries.

2 Secondary research using some well-established published reviews and annotated bibliographies that draw on a wide range of material from the UK, US and New Zealand (E20, D10, D3, A4, F6).

3 Internet searches from key library databases. There are a number of free databases on the web that list research undertaken within children's social care and allied disciplines. Perhaps the most comprehensive of these is Social Care Online, which is produced and maintained by the Social Care Institute of Excellence.

This can be found at:

www.scie-socialcareonline.org.uk

Others websites used were:

research in practice: www.rip.org.uk

Barnado's: www.barnardos.org.uk/resources/research_and_publications.htm

Child Welfare League of America: www.cwla.org

A key task when using internet databases is to decide on a few search terms in advance ('kinship', 'kin', 'family and friends', 'family & friends', etc.) and then use these consistently whichever database you are searching. Some databases also allow you to put in a date filter so that you can search exclusively for recent research.

The information in this review is organised in a logical sequence starting first with the context of family, social, demographic, political, economic and organisational factors that can affect outcomes in kinship care. The next stage goes on to examine outcomes for children in specific areas. This is followed by an analysis of the needs of their carers and birth parents. The final section links to additional research about services and suggests a framework for policy and practice for kinship care.

This review attempts to draw widely on a range of studies and pick out core themes and messages, rather than feed back specifics on a small number of studies. There are very few studies on kinship care that track longitudinal changes over time or set out to compare different types of kinship care. There is a real lack of studies reporting on children's views of kinship care or upon the types of services that have been effective in making kin care work. These are certainly areas for future development.

The published information used in this review (and referenced at the back) have been categorised into eight main types of studies or information:

A UK publications based on primary research on kinship care

B US publications based on primary research on kinship care

C Other studies from abroad (ie, outside UK and US) based on primary research on kinship care

D UK publications based on secondary research, including research reviews and literature reviews

E UK related primary research on children and their families, social work and foster care

F Publications based on secondary research from US and other countries

G General political, theoretical work and training materials

H Government law, policy documents and guidance.

context

In order to understand the impact of kinship care on children, families and service-providers, we have to examine the context in which it is operating. Political, economic, social and demographic factors will shape the ways in which families and state agencies behave and the ways in which social workers, in particular, define and respond to questions of need.

families today

Families in the UK are changing. Children are being born to older parents, grandparents are living longer, one third of children are born outside marriage, and a lone mother heads more than one in five households. One in six fathers live apart from their dependent children (A14). The diversity of family structures is now greater than it has ever been.

Families are more geographically dispersed as the workforce has become increasingly mobile. Despite these changes, surveys illustrate that parents with dependent children still tend to see their relatives more frequently than adults without dependent children. Family members still rely on each other for emotional and practical support when they need it most, and stay in regular contact with their relatives or seek help from them. It is estimated that 5 million people in the UK are unpaid carers (H6). Women who live near their mothers are highly likely to see them on a weekly basis (E41, A14). Grandparents occupy an important role in assisting their adult children to balance work and life responsibilities through the provision of support and child care (A18, A6).

Although family structures have changed, families have remained of central importance in the lives of most people (E41). There is, however, a surprising dearth of information about the ways in which families function. For example, there is scant empirical research on the role that fathers play in families (E9); fathers from minority ethnic groups are even less visible within the available literature (E6). In general, as Utting (D19) noted, there is a 'shortage of data relating to the part grandparents, brothers, sisters, uncles, aunts and cousins play in children's lives'.

Of the 11 million children in England, 4 million are deemed to be vulnerable and living in poverty. It is estimated that in 2005, the last official count, there were 234,700 children in need and the number is steadily increasing (H6). The number of children in public care is also rising – there are now 60,300 looked after children in England (H6), a 22 per cent increase since 1993-94 when 49,500 children were looked after. Sixty-five per cent of children (n=39,300) in public care are subject to care orders; 30 per cent are under single voluntary agreements; and 12.5 per cent have experienced three or more placements during the year. Sixty-eight per cent of children in care are living in foster placements; 13 per cent are living in children's homes and residential schools; 5 per cent are placed for adoption; and 9 per cent of all children in care are placed with parents (H6).

The latest recorded statistics show that 26,400 children are on the child protection register (E13). Children and young people are showing worrying signs of stress. One in ten children under the age of 11 are diagnosed as having a mental health problem (E28). And some groups of children appear to be increasingly criminalised by national policy or identified as 'troubled' or 'troublesome' (E40).

Poverty has risen over the last 15 years with increasing numbers of households falling below the standard poverty line (E14). Rises in poverty hit children and older people the hardest (E19). Research has documented the links between poverty and children coming into public care (D8, D6), particularly children from black and minority ethnic groups who are overrepresented in care (E3) and in the child protection system (D4). Furthermore, studies of the child protection system found that two-thirds of families were living 'on the margins of society' and faced problems more extreme than the serious allegations with which they were confronted (E11).

Poverty is the biggest risk factor in children's lives (D11, E35) and its effects continue to damage children's health and well-being well into adulthood (E19).

> [Poverty is] inexorably correlated with premature delivery, postnatal infant and childhood mortality, malnutrition and ill health, childhood neglect, educational failure, truancy, delinquency, school-age pregnancy and the birth of babies who are victims of premature delivery, postnatal, infant and childhood mortality...
> D11

Inequality, racism and patriarchy all have profound effects on children. There are stark differences in poverty rates according to ethnic group; for example, over half of Bangladeshi, Pakistani and black African children are growing up in poverty (E38) and black and minority ethnic families experience more poverty, ill health and limited access to services (E29, E30).

The government has pledged to eradicate child poverty but in order to do so it has to increase income from employment for poor families, (E38). It has introduced new measures such as Sure Start to tackle the impact of poverty in the early years and it introduced the New Deal to return parents to work, as well as Pathways to Work and legislation to combat discrimination. However, family income still remains a major determinate of a child's health at birth, educational attainment and the type of job they are likely to get in adulthood (E39).

legal and policy context

The inquiry into the death of Victoria Climbié brought about political momentum for change and subsequent legislative reform in the shape of the Green Paper Every Child Matters (H5) and the subsequent Children Act 2004 (H2). The Act is part of a wide strategy to improve the lives of all children and encompasses universal services, as well as services targeted for those most in need.

There are four key strands to the reform programme: better support for parents and carers; early identification of problems and early intervention; greater accountability; and integration of services and workforce reform to develop and retain good-quality child-welfare professionals.

These reforms are being guided and implemented through interagency governance structures legislated for in the Children Act 2004, which provide for directors of children's services, interagency strategic partnerships and Local Safeguarding Children Boards, which are placed on a statutory footing. Front-line services are to become more integrated and services will be co-located through children's centres and extended schools or multidisciplinary teams. Given that the needs of children in kin care are multifaceted, these arrangements could help them. A national common assessment framework and lead professional arrangements are designed to ensure professionals have a common understanding and develop a common language around need, intervention and outcomes.

The legislation is novel in that it sets out five statutory outcomes for children: to be healthy, to stay safe, to enjoy and achieve, to make a positive contribution and to achieve economic well-being. The aim is to ensure a common goal for agencies in relation to children. An outcomes framework is designed to provide a structure for monitoring improvements, inspection and progress towards better outcomes. Therefore in this review the key messages on outcomes for children in kinship care have been organised in line with the new outcomes framework.

The new Act emphasises the importance of partnerships between agencies, which will be supported by new structures and information systems, including ContactPoint – an electronic database of all children that aims to help different professional disciplines share information about children. ContactPoint is a controversial proposal. But despite its potential difficulties and inherent risks, it might provide better information on the number of children in kinship care and private fostering arrangements.

The establishment of a Children's Commissioner was designed to ensure children have a strong independent voice and can influence the services provided to them. Commissioners were also intended to hold children's trusts and strategic partnerships to account on their progress towards improving outcomes for children.

In 2005, the government published its vision for a "competent and confident" children's workforce. This set out four main goals: to recruit more high-quality staff; to retain staff and offer better staff development and career progression; to strengthen interagency working; and to promote strong leadership and management.

The renewed emphasis on early identification of problems and on intervention and better support for parents and carers is at the heart of the Children Act 2004. It reinforces a key assumption of the Children Act 1989 – that children are generally best cared for by their own families.

The Children Act 1989 remains the primary legislation guiding decision making for vulnerable children. The Act intended that 'family' should be interpreted broadly and children helped through supporting families, kin and community (G5). Family life was to be understood as diverse, varying with culture, class, religion and language, and these were significant factors in shaping decisions affecting children (H1, section 22(5)(c)).

The Children Act 1989 was a response to increasing recognition that the removal of children from their families had not produced good outcomes. Research highlighted the growing use of placements with foster carers who were strangers to the child, or in institutions that frequently produced unstable care experiences for children. Children in care were growing up with a sense of loss and displacement (A17, D6).

Black and mixed-heritage children were overrepresented in public care (A25). Children experienced a lack of contact with birth families and placement drift, and insufficient concern was given to child care planning (A17, E36, E17, D6, A2). Those who left care were ill-prepared for family and community life (E51, E24).

The Children Act guidance acknowledged that admission to care had risks attached to it, which should be balanced against risks of children remaining with birth families (H8). In particular, the legislation and accompanying guidance specified that placement with relatives or friends should be considered first for children who could not live with their birth parents.

> If young people cannot remain at home, placement with relatives should be explored before other forms of placement are considered.
> H8

This extended to children who were 'looked after' by the local authority; section 23 (1)(6) lays a duty on the local authority to make arrangements for that child to live with a member of his family unless this would be inconsistent with the child's welfare. 'Family' in this context includes relatives, friends or other people connected to the child.

The box below highlights local authority duties to children in care.

Legal duties likely to impact on kinship care decisions

- duty to place with relative, friend, or person connected with the child (s. 23(6))
- duty to ensure full consultation with the child, carers and family (s. 22 (4))
- duty to involve the child and family in decision making and to consider the child's religion, racial origin and culture (s. 22 (5))
- duty to place children near their home and with siblings (s. 23 (7))
- contact for children with parents and guardians or any other person with whom the child was to live (s. 8 and s. 34 (1)).
(HI)

engaging families – contemporary practice dilemmas

A key challenge facing social work is that it is now delivered through complex bureaucratic structures with increasing attention paid to managerial and procedural mechanisms to deal with children's placement needs. Set within strict agency standards, procedures and courts can lead decision making – with little time or space for social workers to develop partnerships with families (E18, G14, G1). Child protection and risk management have dominated contemporary social work thinking and practice (G13)

Studies of families working with social work systems showed they had limited influence on the nature or quality of services delivered or the way social workers worked with them (E4, A3, E18, A4). The contemporary professional orthodoxy tended to reduce the concept of 'family' to parents, turning the focus on – and blaming – the mother (E16). By contrast, children and parents often perceive their family in broader terms, seeing relations and friends as natural networks and sources of support (A14, E32, A1). Research highlighted a lack of effective partnership practice and an inability to involve caregivers or families in planning and decision making:

Research has consistently stressed the importance of the relationships between social workers and families to achieving good outcomes for children (E48, D7, F29). In this context, social workers may find it difficult to work with kinship care. The necessary partnerships with kinship carers may be difficult to achieve, and class and ethnic differences may have a bigger impact between families and workers than is acknowledged. For example, Beeman and Boisen's (B2) survey suggested that African-American social workers had less difficulty working with kinship care than white social workers.

The unique and family-based nature of kinship care may require agencies to be flexible and responsive to the needs of each particular family. However, control over how – or even whether – placements are supported is located with managers, who are removed from a dialogue of need with families (G7, G6). Practitioners find themselves operating within an organisational structure and culture in which service-users' voices are routinely marginalised, so that the terms and conditions of 'partnerships' between families and professionals could perhaps be better understood as 'limited participation' pre-set by the professional and organisational agenda (G2).

the state of the research

In reviewing the evidence on kinship care, a wide range of practical and methodological difficulties have to be taken into account. This section sets out to highlight some of these and explain their impact on how we might perceive the research and evaluation evidence on kinship care.

constraints and challenges

Few studies have focused exclusively on kin care and its direct effect on children. Many of the research studies that form the body of evidence discussed here originally set out to understand foster care more broadly, from which messages and patterns about family and friends care emerged. Indeed, as Hunt argues in her scoping paper for the Department of Health, there is 'surprisingly little published research which attempts to measure the actual impact of this form of care on children' (E20). This is perhaps particularly the case when looking at outcomes for children who have been abused or neglected and subsequently placed with kin carers.

We know little about ethnicity and kinship care in the UK. Even in the US there is a limited amount of research that comments on how different ethnic groups experience kinship care and what the outcomes are for different children. There are also very few studies on children's views of kinship care and how they experience this type of placement.

Much of the research attempts to judge or 'measure' the effectiveness of kin care compared to non-relative foster care. But attempting to make judgements as to which is 'better' for children is problematic because it underplays the complexities and differences in how these two forms of care are identified, assessed, supported and reviewed. While many of the studies report on kinship foster care, some report on private arrangements that exist outside the fostering system. Research has not always made a clear distinction between the two; many kinship carers are not approved as foster carers (D2). Kinship care is in many ways fundamentally different from foster care with strangers, so a direct comparison may not be as helpful as it first appears (E20, D10).

There are further definitional problems. The broad and varied definitions of family and friends care make it harder to compare or indeed to generalise from the research evidence. We may not be comparing like with like. Different counties or regions have varying ways of defining kinship or family and friends care and use different methods of collecting data. It may be difficult to compare findings from different contexts and local practices. For example, the literature makes little distinction between those kin carers who the child knows prior to placement and those with whom the child is unfamiliar (F6).

This review draws heavily on the research coming out of the US, where there appear to be many more studies. However, caution needs to be exercised; we cannot interpret US findings directly into the UK because the context is very different. In the US, drug abuse and addiction is one if the main reasons for children coming into the care of relatives and kin care is predominately used for African-American families. Furthermore, measures of child development will vary, so different measures may be used to judge the extent of 'emotional disturbance' in children, for example, making it difficult to draw comparisons with other studies (A1).

In her scoping paper, Hunt (E20) describes methodological limitations of research studies into kinship care. In particular she points to the lack of representative samples or control groups in the studies (see below).

Key methodological problems

- use of cross-sectional rather than longitudinal designs
- samples of ongoing rather than completed placements
- lack of baseline measures of comparison so the impact of the placement on the child's well-being cannot be easily determined
- use of global rather than differentiated measures
- wide variation in research approaches and data sources – each having risks of their own methodological bias.

E20

Methodological problems make it hard for the reader to compare directly results from differing studies or to generalise learning from one study to another. The studies tended to judge outcomes by looking at constellations of indicators, clustering them together as evidence rather than having distinct and comparable measures that were specific about the effect on the outcome.

From the US perspective, Gleeson and Hairston (F17) argue there are three main concerns and challenges for research in kinship care:

- how well we balance generalisability (reliability) and depth (validity)
- how clearly we can establish causal relationships given the range of other factors that can impact on placements
- how well we can examine and understand trends over time.

There are other methodological problems. Monitoring social phenomena like child abuse relies on reported incidents, but incidents are, by their nature, often hidden. Hence it is difficult for researchers to find the true extent of these problems. Moreover, definitions and social constructions of what we mean by child abuse vary; what is defined as child abuse in one region or country may not be classed as such in another (this will include also recognition and reporting). So the research on matters such as child safety in family and friends placements (or any other placements) may be harder to judge than first thought.

problems in understanding outcomes

The notion of 'outcome' in child welfare is a very slippery concept and presents a major research challenge. While a number of studies have tried to develop a measure for outcomes, ultimately they tell us little about the actual benefits for children. For example, parental contact or placement stability may not be as beneficial to the child as first assumed (A9); the child may be in a 'stable' placement but the harm it is doing them is hidden, or they may have high levels of contact with a parent but it is emotionally disturbing.

In trying to assess and evaluate outcomes in child welfare it is difficult to identify simple cause and effect relationships that will typically form a part of scientific enquiry in the natural world. It is harder to control the range of factors and variables that have an impact upon the outcome. It has been argued that it may be more realistic to look at 'patterns of benefit and loss' (Whitaker et al quoted in D6) than to try to apply a uni-causal model.

Who defines the important outcomes and how are they best described? For example, would children in kin care describe the outcomes they want or the issues at stake in the same way as an adult observer/researcher seeking to understand outcomes? Much of the research has focused on questions that adults are more interested in – for example, the impact on carers and their needs, or social work agency issues such as placement stability or the management of children's behaviour.

It is striking that when compared to the resources dedicated to other areas of child care research (such as residential care or adoption, which involves broadly similar numbers of children), very few resources have been spent on understanding kinship care. The consequence is a limited knowledge base in this area with the result that theory building and scope of enquiry may still be at a very rudimentary stage of development.

key research messages: outcomes for children

overview

Despite the limitations outlined earlier, some distinct patterns of potential losses and gains for children involved in kinship care are evident, as seen in a number of literature reviews in the last few years (see for example E20, D10, F6, A1).

Overall the research suggests that in the UK, the rest of Europe and the southern hemisphere – and this is also suggested by the more extensive studies in the US – children placed in kinship care broadly appear to do as well as children in non-kin foster care. The evidence is often competing or contradictory but some reoccurring themes do emerge. This section will look in detail at some of these findings.

The research evidence provided here indicates that kinship care appears to produce positive results in areas such as placement stability, maintaining contact with birth parents and the child's connections with their siblings and wider family. These results are more favourable than when children are placed with non-kin carers.

Children appear satisfied growing up with relatives and friends and they see this as more 'natural'. Their identity and positive self-image appear to be supported in these placements. Kinship carers show a strong commitment to the children, the placements can provide the right cultural placement for children, and families tend to be more involved in planning and decision making about the placement.

Measures of outcome on child development, child behaviour, well-being and safety, which might provide more information on the direct impact on the child, are more equivocal and ambiguous. These outcomes have been harder to understand and the research messages are often contradictory.

In relation to the profile of kinship carers (see following chapter), the research is unequivocal: compared to non-kin foster carers, these carers tend to have fewer material resources at their disposal and are more likely to live in poverty. Studies have shown that kin carers tend to be older people, have more health problems and are often single carers. Most commonly they are grandparents; aunts (largely on the maternal side of the family) are the next most common type of kinship carer. Kinship carers get less support and services from social workers and less financial support than non-relative foster carers. Those carers outside the foster care system often get no assistance at all.

The research to date has not directly compared outcomes for children in formal kinship foster care as opposed to placement under a residence or special guardianship order, or for those receiving an allowance or other support services to assist the placement. The research does not tell us whether it is better for children if there is a formal legal arrangement or whether informal agreed arrangements within the family are more effective. It does show us, however, that where arrangements are less formal there is less monitoring and support.

In his review of foster care, Sinclair (D16) invites practitioners and policy makers to think about the following questions in relation to kinship care. Are relative placements routinely considered when a child is fostered?

- Are there policies in place to promote their availability?
- Is there an awareness of advantages and disadvantages?
- Are steps taken to promote advantages and reduce difficulties?
  D16

These may be useful questions to the reader when considering the evidence presented here. The evidence is organised as far as possible in a logical sequence and within the outcomes framework of the Children Act 2004.

be healthy

Key messages

- Both children in kinship and non-kin foster care generally fare worse than the general population of children who grow up with their parents.
- Overall the health and development of children in both kin and non-kin foster placement is similar.
- Most children in kinship and non-kin foster care have some degree of emotional and behaviour problems.
- Children's behaviour is perceived by kinship carers to be less of a problem. Kinship carers may have a more optimistic view or be less likely to report problems than non-kin foster carers.
- Non-kin foster carers tend to have more academic knowledge of child development and more financial and material resources at their disposal.

Children in both kinship care and non-kin foster care appear to have a greater number of health, development, emotional and behavioural problems than in the general population of children (F59).

A review of the National Survey of American Families, which covered 44,000 households, found that children aged 6 to 17 who were involved in the child welfare system (both kinship and non-kinship care) had higher levels of behavioural and emotional problems, and more physical, learning or mental heath problems, than those in parental care (B24).

Using the same data, Billing et al (B10) focused on children in relative care and used measures relating behavioural and emotional problems and school engagement. The study found children living with relatives did worse than those living with parents (see table below). However, children living with relatives had experienced the trauma of separation and were much more likely to be living in poverty, which was one of the main barriers to child well-being.

Comparison of children's problems living with parents and relatives

% of Children	Behavioural and emotional problems (age 6-17)	Suspended from school (age 12-17)	Low school engagement (age 6-17)
Living with parents	7%	13%	20%
Living with relatives	13%	26%	29%

B10

One US study (B58) suggested that children's levels of reported disturbance in kinship care were not significantly different from those of children in two-parent families. Dubowitz et al's (F12) study showed that children in kinship care had clear signs of emotional and behavioural disturbance in 35 per cent of cases. Examining the well-being of adults in a study of 471 women who had lived in kinship care as children, Carpenter and Clyman (B15) found an association with anxiety and unhappiness in later life when compared to the general population of women; however, kin placement was not associated with poor physical health.

Research attempting to compare the health and behaviour of children in kin and non-kin care foster care tends to be inconclusive and sometimes contradictory. In Rowe et al's (A24) UK study of 200 children living with foster parents after three years, just over one-quarter (55 children) were living with relatives. She found lower levels of disturbance in children placed in kinship care, 17 per cent, in contrast to 30 per cent of children in stranger foster care. In a different small-scale study, Hunt (A9) found that 4 of the 11 (36%) children in her sample were showing signs of disturbance as their kin placement developed.

Farmer and Moyers (A5) compared 142 children placed with relatives and friends with 128 children placed with non-relative foster carers. They reviewed 270 case files in 2002 and conducted a follow-up after two years in 2004. They looked at the placements on a range of measures and judged that, overall, they were very similar in their positive effects on the child's well-being. Placements were judged as positive for the child in 73% of kin placements and 79% of non-kin care; as 'adequate' in 14% of kin care and 9% of non-kin placements; and as 'only just managing' with the child's care in 5% of kinship placements and 6% of non-kin foster care. In 8% of kin and 6% of non-kin placements, the placements were seen as detrimental to the child's well-being.

In an intensive study of Scottish families, Aldgate and McIntosh (A1) looked at 30 children living in 24 kinship foster care placements drawn from five local authorities. They found children's physical health to be very good in 23 of the 30 cases, with the remaining group rated as reasonable to good. However, 42 per cent of children were considered to have 'some to high' needs in relation to their emotional and behavioural health. This is higher than in the general population of children. One-third of children in the study showed some level of anxiety linked to past experiences and worries about their future.

In a small sample (in which the definition of kinship care included children placed with fathers with whom they had not previously been living), Harwin et al (A8) found slightly lower health deficits in children in kinship placements: 1 in 14, as opposed to 4 in 15 of those in non-kin foster care and 6 in 19 of those placed for adoption. The study also found that over two-thirds (11 of 15) of children in non-kin foster care were judged to have emotional or behavioural problems, compared to just over half in kinship care (8 of 15); this dropped to 4 of 15 for those children placed for adoption. In a study of 50 young people living with relatives and friends, Broad et al (A3) reported that approximately half the carers described themselves as struggling to cope with difficult behaviour; despite this, nearly all reported positively on some level of improvement in the young person's behaviour.

In their study, Farmer and Moyers (A5) found that mental health support and special educational needs were similar for both kin and non-kin groups; both groups had two-thirds of children with emotional and behavioural problems, ranging from minor to severe. Encouragingly, 77 per cent of children from both types of placement showed improvements in behaviour during the placement. In this study, the level of children's behaviour problems prior to placement was similar for children in kin and unrelated care. However, slightly more kin placements broke down because of children's behaviour (33% compared to 23% with non-related foster carers). This may be due to the lack of placement support or to increasing difficulties because of the carers' age or ill health.

Several US studies have reviewed the characteristics of children placed in kinship care and non-kin foster care and have found that, overall, health status, educational needs and behavioural problems are similar (F5, B20, F23). Interestingly, both Starr et al (F46) and Solomon and Marx (B58) found that boys in kinship care had more emotional and behavioural difficulties than girls. Chipungu et al (B17) suggest that children placed with relatives are doing somewhat better in terms of health needs.

Benedict et al (B5) conducted a series of interviews with children in kin and non-kin placements. They found that children in kin placements had a statistically significant lower incidence of problems in terms of mental health, behaviour and other problems when compared to children growing up in non-kin foster care (see table below). However, the study also indicated that the children had fewer problems prior to placement. This was supported by Berrick et al (F5) who also found fewer behaviour problems in children in kinship care compared to non-kin foster care for children aged between 4 and 15.

Comparison of children's problems in kin and non-kin placement

Identified problem in placement	Behaviour	Running away	Trouble with the law	Mental health
Kinship care	53%	22%	17%	39%
Non-kin placement	79%	37%	27%	71%

B5

Iglehart (F23) found that 33 per cent of kin-placed children had behaviour problems noted on case records, but this was similar to children in non-relative foster care. However, kin-placed children had notably fewer mental health problems and showed greater adjustments to their new care arrangement. The researchers suggested the availability of a familiar carer at a time of crisis may have psychological benefits to the child.

Brooks (B12) studied 600 caregivers in the US in a variety of settings and found that substance-exposed children tended to have more behaviour problems and that kin placements appeared more effective for non-substance-exposed children. Grandparents who are carers appear more likely to suffer depression than younger carers and this can lead to parenting problems, which in turn is linked to adolescent substance abuse (A23).

While children's behaviour in kinship care may appear less problematic, it may be they arrive with less severe development and behaviour problems than those who go to non-kin care (E20). This is a significant question that needs further exploration. It is possible, too, that kinship carers are more optimistic about 'their' child's development or do not recognise signs of behaviour or emotional problems as quickly – or they may be less likely to report difficulties than non-kin foster carers. Indeed, Laws (A12) noted that kinship carers had generally positive views of children's well-being while the children they were looking after did have notable emotional and behaviour problems.

Timmer et al (B61), in a study of 102 kinship and 157 non-kin placements, found that non-kin foster carers rated their foster children's behaviour problems as more severe than did kin caregivers. Interestingly, they also rated themselves as less stressed than kin caregivers.

Kinship carers may be given less information about the child's problems, either from the birth parents or the social workers involved, than non-kin carers. In a small study (12 cases), Gibson (B31) found that after becoming kinship caregivers, children's grandparents became aware of problems in the child's behaviour that were previously unknown to them. They reported that they were concerned about the grandchild's emotional and physical well-being.

A key methodological problem is that medical records are often incomplete or unavailable for children placed with kin carers (B30) so it is hard to compare results with those children in non-kin care whose records are more accessible to researchers.

Only one study appears to have examined outcomes for children who were in kin and non-kin foster care to the point where they left care and became adults. The research showed no significant difference between the two groups in terms of school completion, employment, mental or emotional health (B5).

stay safe

Key messages

- Kinship care appears to provide children with the same level of safety from abuse or neglect as non-kin foster care.
- Kinship placements generally have less professional support, services and monitoring; this is likely to affect the research findings.
- Paradoxically, one of the key professional concerns about kinship care is child safety, yet there is limited evidence to support this concern, though research in this area is surprisingly underdeveloped.
- Kinship care placements appear as stable and often more stable than non-kin foster care.
- Compared to non-kin foster care, kinship placements tend to last longer and children are less likely to experience multiple placement moves.
- Kin placements may offer a greater sense of security and belonging to children.
- Children in kin care are far more likely to have a relationship with their carers prior to placement and that relationship is more likely to continue into adulthood
- When children in care move, those in kinship care are more likely to go to another relative than those in non-kin foster care.
- Kinship care increases the likelihood of the child remaining in the same cultural and ethnic environment and relatives can assist with identity issues.
- A proportionally larger number of kinship placements appear to be with families from black and minority ethnic families (particularly in the US, although some UK evidence refutes this).
- Kinship care appears to enable children to maintain a wider set of relationships and connections to their family and community than does placement in non-kin foster care.
- Children are more likely to be placed with siblings in kin care than if they are placed in non-relative care.

safeguarding

Given that child safety and risk management are central concerns of modern-day social work, there is a surprising dearth of information on the question how safe is kinship care? While there are a number of enduring professional concerns about child safety in kinship care, to date there is little evidence to support those concerns. Concerns about intergenerational abuse feature strongly in the minds of social workers (B30, A4) and have a significant influence on decision making. In a study involving interviews with 40 social workers and five social work managers, concern about child safety was the single most important and recurring theme as to why social workers would worry about placing a child in kinship care (A4).

When looking at research in child welfare it is worth remembering that children who are living away from parents are generally more vulnerable and have extra needs compared with the general population of children. Indeed Dubowitz et al (B21) found that kin and non-kin foster carers were both more likely to be accused of abusing a child in their care than in the general population of parents. While there is scant research on the question of child safety in kin care, the absence in the wider evidence of any notable increased risk to children in these placements may be significant (D2, E20).

Given the limitations described, kinship placements appear to provide the same level of safety to children as placement with non-kin foster carers (B6, B28).

Benedict et al (B5) found substantiated reports of abuse were actually more likely to occur in cases involving non-kin foster parents, although the differences were not thought to be statistically significant. In a sample study of foster homes by Zuravin et al (F61), children appeared more vulnerable to abuse in non-kin foster care, where they were twice as likely to have a confirmed report of child abuse compared to care with relatives. Farmer and Moyers' (A5) found allegations were founded against kin carers and non-kin carers equally in four per cent of cases. Kin carers, however, experienced more unsubstantiated allegations (4%) than non-related carers (1%) and the authors argue there is a need for ongoing monitoring.

Broad's (D2) study involving 50 young people aged between 11 and 25, noted that young people in kinship care felt safe and talked about the importance of 'being rescued' from local authority care. Wilson (B65) researched children's experiences and interviewed children about being in kin and non-relative foster care and found that both groups of children equally reported feeling safe. Children in Poland reported feeling safe when placed with relatives (C13).

In contrast to the above, the General Accounting Office (F14) findings suggest that kin caregivers may be less likely to enforce protective restrictions with respect to parental visits than non-kin foster carers. Rodning et al (F40) found in a very small sample of children, who had been placed with kin by state agencies initially, the majority of children actually ended up being cared for by their birth mothers without the authorities' knowledge.

A study examining child-welfare workers' perspectives on informal kinship care (ie, care that was not formally screened, sanctioned and trained by the agency) found that US social workers felt that in one-third of non-approved kinship placements, standards fell below those they regularly achieved in foster homes (B7). The authors suggest that better screening, training and education for kinship carers are necessary to raise standards of care.

Kinship placements generally have less professional support and monitoring and this may affect research findings in this area. The lack of professional involvement could hide abuse as it is less likely to be discovered. Less monitoring of placements, combined with the possibility of greater worker 'tolerance' of reported transgressions within kin care, may produce inaccurate results (B57). It is worth noting that a lack of support from professionals, allied with fewer services, may increase the risk of child harm or neglect in kin care – but to date there is little strong evidence to support this proposition.

placement stability

A key recurring theme of the early research is that kinship placements offer children good levels of stability in their placement. Research studies in the UK that set out to examine foster care began to identify this feature in kinship care. Differences emerged between those children placed with relatives and those who were fostered with strangers. Rowe et al (A24) found kin care held qualitative advantages over children placed with strangers, particularly the role grandparents would play.

> To our considerable surprise, our data shows that children fostered by relatives seem to be doing better in virtually all respects than those fostered by others.
> (A24)

The study noted that children with relatives had a 'high level of placement stability' and were half as likely as children in non-kin foster care to have placement moves. These kinship placements tended to involve care for 'older children with more complex problems but still achieved better results'. More than ten years on from this study, Thoburn (D17) found fostering with relatives to be more successful on a range of measures when compared to care with non-relatives.

Further studies in the UK reported lower disruption rates (at about 10% in kin care) with fewer moves than in non-kin foster care (A2, A17). Placement with kin was seen to provide more positive placement histories for children on a range of measures (D18).

Broad et al's (D2) study found that 46 per cent of 50 placements were relatively stable, lasting between one and five years. Their figures suggest 'a pattern of "longer-term stability" for the majority of the family and friends placements studied'. Farmer and Moyers (A5) also found that a significantly higher number of kin placements last longer (72%) when compared with non-kin foster care (54%). The average length of kin placement was four years and nine months, which compared to three years and eleven months for non-kin foster care (this was partly because children move from short to long-term placements and into adoption from non-kin foster care, but not from relatives). Aldgate and McIntosh (A1) found one-third of children, in a sample of 30, stayed for most of their childhoods and children aged 5 to 11 had spent at least three years in kin placement.

Kinship placements appear more durable despite the significant hardships kinship carers face (see the section, 'Carers' strengths and needs', p55). For example, Hunt (A9) researched children who were subject to care proceedings and examined outcomes for those placed with relatives four years on. Although it was a small sample, she found that kin placements had continued and compared favourably with non-kin, long-term foster care. This was despite children's previous histories of poor parenting and parental hostility to the placement. Interestingly, placement under a care order had the highest breakdown rate; by contrast, placements where only residence orders were used had not broken down.

Grandparents have a significant role in caring for their grandchildren. Richards (A22) found that of 180 grandparents caring for children with and without court orders, 21 per cent had cared for the child/children for ten years or more; 15.5 per cent for between five and ten years; and 63.5 per cent for less than five years. Harwin et al (A8) found that placements involving ethnic minority children in kin care were less likely to break down.

Recent UK studies are more equivocal about placement stability. Sinclair et al (E46) looked in detail at 476 foster placements out of a survey of 600. The study did not specifically set out to examine kin foster care but found disruption rates at 38 per cent, which is a much higher incidence than in earlier studies. This study found no clear differences between kin and non-kin foster care. The study concluded that overall they 'did not find the outcomes were on average better or worse in placements with relatives'. This finding was supported by another large-scale UK study by Farmer and Moyers (A5) who found disruption rates between kin and non-kin foster carers the same at 13 per cent.

In reviewing the existing research evidence, Hunt (E20) notes that there has been a recurring finding on disruption rates of approximately 30 per cent for kinship placements (B59, F23, B40, E46).

Studies from the US also show kinship placements to be stable (B13, B25, F12, B45, B5, F14, B63). These placements tend to last longer and children experience fewer changes of placement than with traditional foster carers (F5, B20, B27). Kin care children appear significantly less likely to experience multiple placements and this is a recurring theme in the literature (B3, B5, F8, F23, B19).

Many kin carers say they have made a lifetime commitment to the children and plan to care for them into adulthood (F5, F53). Aldgate and McIntosh (A1) found that while two-thirds of the carers reported that 23 of 30 children would be with them into adulthood, most expected it would be 'forever' and the child was seen as a permanent member of the family. The personal commitment that carers make to that particular child, and the quality of the relationship with the child, may be the most important factor in the durability of these placements.

A random sample of 516 children aged between birth and five years old entering the public care system in New York City found that children placed in kinship care had fewer placement changes than those in non-kin foster care (F60). And in a study looking at the experiences of younger children, Berrick (F4) found that 53 per cent of children in stranger foster care experienced at least three placement changes compared to 30 per cent of children in kin care. This finding was supported by Webster et al (B63), who conducted a longitudinal study of children in care over eight years; just under 30 per cent of children in kin care experienced three or more placements, compared to 50 per cent of children in non-kin care.

In Sweden, Sallnas et al (C9) studied a foster care cohort of 776 young people over five years. They found that between 30 and 37 per cent of all placements terminated prematurely, with the lowest rates of breakdown being in kinship care and in secure units. In a study of placement disruption, analysing a cohort of 1,084 children in Australia, James (B41) found kinship placements were more stable and noted that, overall, 20 per cent of all placement changes were due to behaviour problems; the highest risk related to the first 100 days of placement. Placements have higher levels of breakdown for boys than girls (E21) and disruption is more likely for the older child (A8, F1, B63).

relationships, attachment and identity

Farmer and Moyers (A5) found that the vast majority of children placed in both kinship (97%) and non-kin foster care (93%) were attached to an adult; only three per cent in kin care and seven per cent in non-kin foster care had little or no attachment to an adult. Research generally reports positively on the quality of relationships in kin care (E20, C13) and Altshuler (F2) found greater depths of bonding.

Children in kin care are far more likely to have had a previous relationship with their carers (F32, F14) and there is evidence that relatives or friends are more likely to expect children to form close personal relationships with them than non-kin carers (B13, A1). Indeed placement may strengthen child and carer relationships that already exist (F31) and reduce the emotional trauma of the effects of separation from parents (F12).

Children appear to experience a greater sense of security when placed within their family networks (B25, F23). As grandmothers – followed by aunts – are the most frequent caregivers, the child is usually building on an existing relationship. This provides continuity in the child's experience (F5, B16). When children are asked about the future, studies have shown many expect that they will be living in the same kinship care placement over the forthcoming months (F1). In interviews with 11 children in kin care, Doolan et al (A4) found that all but one described their placement as long-term and stable.

In contrast, however, Gaudin and Sutphen (B28) found no difference in affection with respect to kin and non-kin foster care. Moreover, where relationships are not especially close, placements were seen as more at risk. Testa and Shook-Slack (F50) found that in placements in which a caregiver reported a poor relationship with the child, these were judged to be nearly three times as likely (283%) to terminate than those in which the carer's relationship with the child was judged as good. Clearly, then, this must form a central question in any assessments social workers make of kinship care placements.

When kin-placed children did move, they were more likely than children in non-kin foster care to move to another relative (F7, F8), but they were also slower to re-unify to parents (A15, F7). Staying within the family may minimise the impact of loss and change, but we don't know from research whether it is better for children to move between the care of strangers or within kin care. Testa and Shook-Slack (F50) showed that of 983 children, those in family and friends care were slightly more likely to be placed with another relative if they moved – 16 per cent, compared to 14 per cent in non-kin foster care. Pemberton (C7) looked at traveller communities and found evidence of children moving within family and community networks. However, concern has been raised that children can drift in family care without monitoring, being moved from one relative to another (F13). Farmer and Moyers (A5) found that children placed with relatives were more likely to have had a previous relative placement – and if the placement ended they were more likely to go to another relative. Likewise, children in non-kin placements were more likely to move between non-kin placements if a placement ended.

There is a growing recognition of the importance of identity and continuity in children's lives. Families provide the most enduring relationships for children and young people, even those who cannot live with their parents (A25, A17, D6, E8). Children placed with extended family are more likely to experience this continuity of relationships (F35) and kin care appears to help maintain a child's sense of identity and self-esteem (D17), which flows from knowing family history and culture. Children in kinship care often have more information about their parents than children placed in stranger foster care (A24).

Studies in the UK have shown that black and minority ethnic group carers who were grandparents placed importance on handing on to children cultural traditions, including language and religious beliefs (A22). Broad et al (D2) found that in all but one case, the ethnicity of the carers matched that of the child or young person. Staying within a kinship group can help to maintain important cultural and religious traditions. Wheal (D22) argues that this reduces the traumatic impact of separating from parents, as it is not also accompanied by a separation from culture – ethnicity, language, religion, traditions and class. Remaining in a familiar cultural and religious group can also help to reinforce positive images and experiences of self, family and culture (E42). Even for children who are adopted, research has shown that if they retain links with their families of origin, then placements may be less likely to disrupt and children benefit from improved self-esteem and a clearer self-concept (E44).

There are proportionately more kin caregivers in black and minority ethnic communities in the US (F5, F21) and this has implications for the way kin placements are identified, assessed and supported. Research suggests a professional lack of understanding of needs and a lack of culturally appropriate services for different black and minority ethnic communities, so this is a critical area for development (D10).

In the UK, data on ethnicity has not been routinely collected, but one study did show high proportions of kin carers in African and African-Caribbean communities (E22). Two studies in London boroughs (A3, A4) showed a high proportion of black and minority ethnic families involved in kin care. By contrast, a recent large study outside London (A5) found that black and minority ethnic children appear to be placed less often with relatives than are white children, with significantly more black and minority ethnic children (60%) placed with non-relative carers.

Black children are more likely to enter the care system (E1, E2) and they are also more likely to remain in care long-term if they are placed with relatives of the same culture and ethnicity (E5). Children can have their cultural identities affirmed and relatives may provide them with survival skills for dealing with racism in day-to-day life.

Kinship care appears to enable children to maintain a wider set of relationships and connections to their family and community than does placement in non-kin foster care, although there are some contradictory findings (B14, B59).

Children's relationships and connections with their siblings and friends are important (E53). Children in kin care appear more likely to be placed with their brothers and sisters when compared to those in non-kin foster care (A11). Harwin et al (A8) found 9 of 13 children in kinship care were placed with at least one sibling, while Hunt and Macleod (E21) found that of 15 children placed with kin, only two sets of siblings had been separated. Although Kosenen (A10) found a much lower percentage of kin care children placed with siblings (43%), this is still a higher percentage than the number of siblings being placed with strangers.

Maintaining links is 'important to most young people' and that includes links with both parents and siblings (D2). Broad et al found that for children, keeping in touch with people and friends whom they had known in an earlier life was 'important in feeling settled' and 'carers were seen as central to helping them maintain these links'.

O'Brien's (C6) Irish study found 62 per cent of children placed with kin had siblings placed with them or with other members of their extended family. In a sample of 37 children in one London borough, two-thirds of kin placements involved siblings being placed together, either by joining a sibling group or joining half-siblings; only five of the 37 children were placed as the only child in a household (A4). By contrast, another UK study (A5) found similar proportions of children placed with siblings in kin (53%) and non-kin (52%) placements. This matches work of Scannapicco ct al (B56) who found little difference between kin and non-kin placement of siblings, with siblings being separated in three of every five placements. Interestingly Farmer and Moyers found that more children in kin care (22%) than in non-kin care (6%) were the lone child in the home; these lone-child placements were significantly more likely to end.

Sinclair et al (E46) argue that placing siblings together has a number of benefits for children; they can help each other in understanding their identity, support each other, and maintain knowledge of their own family and heritage.

International evidence suggests that contact with siblings (B43, B17) and other family and friends (F14) may be facilitated by kinship placements. Shlonsky and Berrick (B57) found sibling groups were placed together with relatives much more often and that relatives were more willing to accept sibling groups.

Interestingly, tension between the child and other children in the household was much more common when children were placed with non-kin carers (76%) than with kinship carers (45%) (A5). This may be because relationships pre-existed or because children feel more integrated and part of a family.

enjoy and achieve

Key messages

- Children involved with the child welfare system are more likely to have lower levels of school engagement compared to children in parental care.
- Overall comparisons of education performance between children in kinship care and non-kin care are equivocal and contradictory.
- Educational problems for children in kinship care are similar for children in stranger foster care.
- Kin caregivers may have slightly more difficulty getting children to school but report fewer school problems to social workers.
- Children in kinship care appear to be more likely to remain within or closer to their own community and are more likely to stay in touch with friends and school.
- There are few studies of children's views of kinship care.
- Kinship care appears more likely to promote satisfaction from children in their placement than does placement with strangers.
- Children report feeling happier and more loved in kinship care.
- Kin care appears to provide children with a greater sense of belonging within their own family networks.
- Children are aware of conflicts and issues relating to their parents.

education

There is a raft of research evidence that has highlighted the poor levels of school engagement and performance for children in care (D23) and that this area deserves more attention from social workers than it currently gets (E10, H7).

Children involved with the child welfare system are more likely to have lower levels of school engagement compared to children in parental care and are more likely to be suspended or excluded from school (B24). However, one study (B58) found that while children in kinship care (living with grandparents) did less well academically than those living with two-parent families, they achieved more than those living with a single parent.

In the UK, Rowe et al's (A24) study of long-term foster care had more positive findings, with 81 per cent of children achieving at least average levels at school and only 15 per cent considered by their social workers to be underachieving. Farmer and Moyers (A5) suggest a more depressing figure, with about one-third of children performing below their ability in both kin and non-kin placements. This supports an earlier finding by Harwin et al (A8), whose study found that just under a third of children (29%) in non-kin foster care were judged to have educational problems.

The Broad et al (D2) study found that almost all the 13 carers interviewed felt positive about the placement improving the young person's behaviour and educational achievements, and young people thought one of the benefits of kinship care was getting support with education. In their Scottish study, Aldgate and McIntosh (A1) found that 22 of 24 carers felt their child had done very well in school. Carers reported about 30 per cent of children as showing slower progress at school, the main reason being problems with concentration. In addition, Doolan et al (A4) found children reported school to be a very important point of stability in their lives.

The evidence on the educational performance of children in kinship and non-kin care is inconclusive. Some studies (F5, F23) report children in kinship care doing better than those in non kin-foster placements. However, between one-third and one-half of children studied in kin care (F5, B55) appear to be achieving less than would be expected for children of their age when compared to the general population of children.

Some studies report slight differences in educational achievement between kin and non-kin foster care (B56, B13), while other studies have found no difference at all (B5). By contrast Chipungu et al (B17) report children in kin care doing worse. Farmer and Moyers (A5) found school attendance levels were similar for both groups (78% in kin care and 84% in non-kin placements).

Worrall (C14), in her small study in New Zealand, identified a significant number of children who had been excluded from school. She found the majority of kin-care placed children had not performed well academically and presented difficult behaviour in school. Studies suggest similar levels of school behaviour problems between kin and non-kin placed children (F5, B20, F23). Though kinship caregivers appear to have slightly more difficulty getting children to school, they are less likely to report problems to their social workers about these difficulties (19%) than non-kin foster carers (44%) (A24).

Significantly more kin placements appear to be closer to the family home (66%) when compared to placements with stranger carers (46%) (Farmer and Moyers (A5). In the UK, fewer children placed with relatives or friends changed school when they moved to a kinship placement (38%), compared to children who moved to a stranger foster care placement (51%) (A5, E45). Aldgate and McIntosh (A1) found that 13 of 30 children had changed school as a result of their placement, but only four changed school while in placement.

Children in kin care are as likely (or more likely) to remain in the same community or area than children placed with non-kin carers (B7, F49, G15, F14, C1). They are also at least as likely to remain at the same school (B13) and in other studies were more likely to do so (F14). This is not a consistent finding, however. Chipungu et al (B17) found that children in kin placements were actually more likely than those in stranger placements to live outside of the state. And in Australia, Hannah and Pitman (C3) noted that in half the kin placements assessed, children lived beyond state boundaries.

children's views

Historically, studies involving children's perceptions of outcomes have been few and far between. It is more common for adult perceptions of children's needs to dominate research projects. To date, children's perspectives and priorities have not been given sufficient importance by researchers (E31).

The reluctance to involve children as active participants in the research process may say more about adult anxieties than it does about children's ability to take part and contribute (G11). There is a need to involve children more readily in the design, implementation, analysis and dissemination of research in kinship care if measures such as 'satisfaction' and 'happiness' are to become more meaningful. This is important, not least because research shows that if children in foster care are motivated to make their placement succeed, then this is a strong predictor of the outcome of placement (E45).

Kinship care seems to be more likely than placement with strangers to promote satisfaction from children and engender a commitment to their placement (F58, F8). Children in these placements appear to experience a greater sense of belonging because they remain connected with family members who they know and who know them. Children in kin placements are more likely to view their role as an integral part of their kinship family (B37, B43) compared to those in stranger foster care.

The studies that have interviewed children about their views of placements are few in number and involve small samples. Despite these limitations, some themes are emerging. Wilson (B65) researched children's experiences of kin and non-kin care and found that children in kin care were more likely to say they felt happy. A greater percentage of children in kin care also reported that they 'always felt loved' (94% compared to 82% in non-kin foster care).

In a study involving interviews with just four kin-placed children, Smith et al (C10) found that the children reported being 'happy' with those they were living with and spoke positively about their caregivers. Similarly, Rowe et al (A24) found that children reported positive feelings about their carers and had a sense of security about their futures. Children also report frequent experiences of fun and achievement (A1). Doolan et al (A4) used semi-structured interviews to gather qualitative data from 11 children, whose ages were spread equally between eight and 18; all the children reported positively on their placement and carers and on the quality of their care and relationships.

In a study involving the views of social workers, Beeman and Boisen (B2) found 70 per cent of social workers considered that children in kin placements demonstrated a stronger sense of belonging than those in non-kin foster care. Only seven per cent of workers thought children might feel more insecure as a result of being in kin care as opposed to foster care.

Doolan et al (A4) used semi-structured interviews to gather the views of a sample of 40 social workers and five team managers. Only a third of the social workers saw the child's wishes and feelings as a key factor influencing assessment and decisions about where the child should live.

Using open-ended questions with a small sample of six children, Altshuler (F2) found that children adjusted well to kinship care, although they reported being sad at leaving their parents. Children liked the discipline and stability of their placements and were excited about their future.

In their study Kith and Kin, Broad et al (A3) conducted interviews with 22 young people, who described the positives of kinship care as:

- feeling loved, valued and cared for
- belonging within your own family, feeling settled and not being moved around
- good to be with people you know
- sustaining a sense of who you are and staying in contact with family and friends
- feeling safe
- being listened to
- not going into the care of strangers.

A3

On the negative side, young people in the same study also reported that they did not like the restrictions imposed on their freedom by carers, and they were aware of the financial hardship experienced by their caregiver. While children do identify problems and tensions in kin care, it seems they place fundamental value on the importance of being wanted and loved within the family circle. Farmer and Moyers (A5) found that where a child was the only child in a kinship placement, children described the loneliness of living with elderly relatives and having few other children in their locality. Interestingly, these lone placements were more likely to end than placements that involved other children living in the kinship home.

O'Brien (C5) found that children remained very aware of their own parents and their problems and often worried about them. This is a common pattern for all children in care (A1). O'Brien found that all but one child living with relatives wished to be with their own parents; however, the children had also come to terms with the fact that this was unlikely to happen and so saw themselves staying with carers until they were adults.

make a positive contribution

Key messages

- Children's participation and partnership with families are closely associated with good outcomes for children but are hard to achieve in day-to-day social work.
- Children and their families want to participate and are more satisfied with outcomes when they do.
- Children want information about their circumstances and choices.
- Children want to see more of their social worker and to have a reliable relationship with them; this helps children make decisions.
- Children do not necessarily conform to stereotypical or assumed images of family when defining their closest kin.
- Children and extended families participate in day-to-day decision making far more with kinship care placements.
- Family Group Conferences are a positive way to enhance child and family participation in the kinship placement planning process.
- Family Group Conferences are an effective way of ensuring that children's voices are heard in planning and decision making.

participation

Research in the UK shows that the participation of children and their families in social work activity is still underdeveloped (E11, E18, E4, E31). Practice has tended to be orientated to agency needs, requirements and standards rather than child and family participation, but when partnership is achieved it leads to far higher levels of user satisfaction and agreement over plans for children (E48, D7, E27, E47).

Kinship care can be understood as one means of empowering families, involving users and encouraging anti-oppressive practice

(G4). In this context, there is some evidence to suggest that families can have more influence over kinship placements (C8, F34). Good working relationships between social workers, children, parents and caregivers will have a positive impact on outcomes for children (F29). Therefore developing effective family participation practice is an important element of improving decision making and planning for children in kin care (G10).

In (A5), Farmer and Moyers found that 86 per cent of placements with kin were made because relatives were already caring for the children or offered to do so. Also, children actually initiated nine per cent of kin placements; social workers appeared to initiate only four per cent of placements when kin had not made the first contact. Aldgate and McIntosh (A1) found that of 30 children in kin care placements, 8 were initiated by relatives taking emergency action, 9 placements were arranged by the social worker, and the majority – 13 placements – came about by mutual agreement between the child, carers and parents, with social workers sometimes involved. As with the previous study, albeit to a lesser extent, it is children and families who are making kin foster placements more often than professional agencies.

Children need a range of supports to help them participate in decisions. Doolan et al 2004 found from 11 kin placed children that they:

- wanted to see more of their social worker and to have a reliable relationship with them
- needed more involvement in decisions
- wanted information about their circumstances and choices
- wanted to keep in touch with family and friends
- wanted proper financial support for their carers.

family group conferences

Research into Family Group Conferences (FGCs), a model of family decision making, shows high levels of satisfaction with participation in the placement planning process, for children and adult family members alike (E25, E26, E27). The national (UK) study on FGCs showed that children offered an FGC were more likely (than with orthodox methods) to be placed with extended family and that the placement was more likely to be stable (E12). This is significant also because children tend to define their family and friendship network more broadly than professionals do (E32) and so would include more family members.

FGCs have been slow to be implemented in the UK and studies imply a resistance to their use (E27, G8). There are concerns about the willingness of the extended family to adhere to plans, allied to a lack of follow-through and service delivery by social workers and other agencies post-conference (E26).

In New Zealand, the involvement of extended family was seen to increase the support to the original caregivers (F19) and this pattern appears to be replicated in the UK (F11). Extended family members were also far more likely to be involved in offering support to the child and kin than with traditional approaches. Marsh and Crow (E27) looked at 80 FGCs in the UK; families offered some level of support in 94 per cent of cases, and in 31 per cent of cases families offered to look after the children for at least some period of time.

Research in New Zealand, where FGCs have been running longest, has indicated a significant reduction of children in public care and the courts (C4, F37), although there have been problems with official record keeping, so comparisons have been problematic. However, on the basis of the existing research from New Zealand, Thornton (F52) concludes:

> Families are more involved than ever in making decisions and taking responsibility for their children. Fewer children are being separated from their family or whanau [Maori for 'family'] than for many years.
> F52

Research in the US has generally supported the finding that FGCs increase the use of kinship placements (F9, F55); Ticomb and LeCroy found that placement with relatives increased by two thirds following a FGC. However, by contrast, Gunderson et al (F18) found an increase of children living with their parents and a corresponding decrease of those living with relatives.

Research shows children participate more readily in FGCs than other forms of meeting and have a greater say about their placement needs (E26). The FGC allows family to make decisions in a way that reflects their traditions and culture. FGCs have been practiced in a wide range of different cultural contexts and surveys have shown their adaptability (B49). Importantly, FGCs offer a culturally sensitive model, respectfully reinforcing the importance of identity, culture and relationships within families (E6).

achieve economic well-being

Key messages

- Children in kinship placements are more likely than those in non-kin foster care to grow up in material and financial poverty, which has a significant impact on health and well-being.
- Housing, overcrowding and a lack of material resources is a significant pattern in kinship care.
- Very few longitudinal studies have mapped children in kinship care to adulthood.
- In transition to independence, the importance of family is often overlooked by professionals.
- Children knowing they can return to or get support from kinship carers may be an important variable that makes placements work.

Children in kin care are much more vulnerable to the effects of poverty, particularly when compared to children in non-kin foster care. In the US, Billing et al (B10) found children in kinship care much more likely to be living in poverty. In the UK, Farmer and Moyers (A5) found evidence of financial difficulty in 75 per cent of kin placements but in only 13 per cent of non-kin foster care placements. Doolan et al (A4) found financial pressures in all 23 placements they studied. Statistically, kinship care puts children at higher risk of living in poverty, which can have a profound effect on their life chances (B23). Grandparents – the most common kin carers – report having to make financial sacrifices in 85 per cent of cases; 72 per cent described experiencing financial hardship, with 36 per cent having to give up work (A22). This is a recurring and consistent finding.

In the Scottish study, Aldgate and McIntosh (A1) found housing problems and overcrowding. Of 30 children 13 shared a room, including eight who shared with an adult. This would not be acceptable in foster care. Doolan et al (A4) also identified the problem of overcrowding. Altshuler (F2) studied the well-being of 62 randomly sampled children in kin care, and found a significant link between child well-being and mothers not having housing problems and the kin caregiver's own health and ability to provide care.

For some groups of children in kinship care the situation may be improving. Main et al (B46) looked at data in the USA, over a six-year period, tracking the social characteristics of 44,000 households and then analysing the data relating to children. They found the financial circumstances of children in kinship care had improved significantly over recent years (between 1997 and 2002). Children in formal kinship foster care experienced the most dramatic improvements, with numbers living in poverty being halved. The proportion of children living in poverty in private kinship care also fell, but not as steeply, to 30 per cent (compared to 18 per cent in formal kinship foster care). Main et al argue that children in formal kin care have now increased their living standards close to that of children living with parents. They argue that increased regulation and support for kinship care has improved matters significantly. Their study suggests, however, that many kinship families don't know their entitlements, so when kinship care is supported by child welfare agencies it does much better in terms of tackling the effects of poverty and providing better practical and material support.

The evidence above raises questions about social workers promoting the use of residence and special guardianship orders for kinship care. While this is accepted good practice, because it involves carers making a long-term commitment to the child (although the evidence suggests many are already strongly committed), it also presents the risk of agencies withdrawing material, financial and practical support to the placement, potentially reducing the opportunities for good outcomes.

There are very few studies that have tracked outcomes for children leaving kinship care into adulthood. However, one longitudinal study that did track outcomes into adulthood (B5) conducted interviews with

214 adults who were previously in care as children (40% in kinship care). Both those who grew up in kinship care and those who grew up in non-kin foster placements had broadly similar adult outcomes in terms of education, current employment, physical and mental health, risk-taking behaviours, stresses and support networks.

Research suggests that large numbers of young people who leave care do so ill-prepared for family and community life (E24). One study that examined young people leaving care to independence (A16) found that while the majority of social workers felt care leavers were unprepared emotionally for leaving care, there was insufficient work to engage the extended family and child's community networks in their future support. The study found:

- Family for most young people could be interpreted broadly. Care leavers could often describe a wide family network (average over 20), but most had infrequent contact with them.
- Social workers were aware of less than half the family members identified as key kin by young people; 41 of the 43 young people in the study described the most important or influential person to them on leaving care as key kin (in less than 25 per cent of cases was this the young person's mother, yet social work tended to focus on mothers).
- Family information on care leavers' case files was limited and frequently out of date or inaccurate; in 70 per cent of reviews held before the young person left care, no family member was present.
- Social workers expected that young people would receive increased support from families once they left care, but this did not always materialise in practice.

The study suggests that more work should be done to understand and engage the young person's family and friendship network before they leave care and suggests that interventions should be targeted on the child's connections, networks and family relations (see Figure 2).

Figure 2:

targeting interventions and support

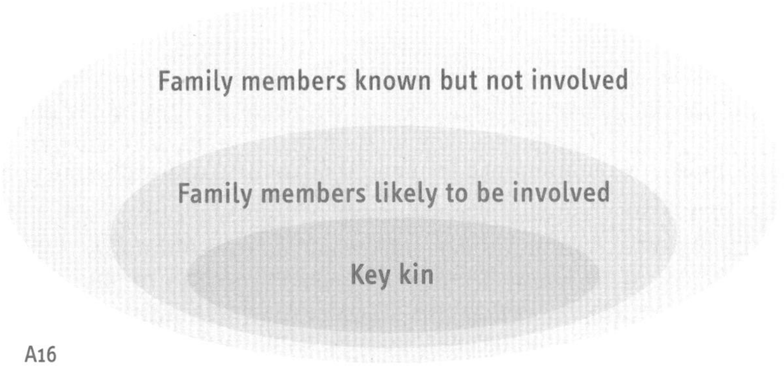

Family members known but not involved

Family members likely to be involved

Key kin

A16

Iglehart (F24) found that children in kin and non-kin placements were more likely to worry about their future than the general population of children, but that 50 per cent of those in kinship care expected to go on living with their carers once discharged from care, compared to 13 per cent of those in non-kin placements. The author suggests that one of the significant reasons kinship care makes a difference is the continued availability of the relative's home as a source of support to the young person as they move to adulthood and independent living.

findings related to outcomes: contact

Key messages

- In most cases, children and kin carers want contact with parents and other family members.
- Contact with parents and other family members occurs more 'naturally' in kin care and contact is far more frequent than in non-kin care.
- Contact can improve placement stability and provide some continuity for children.
- A significant number of contact arrangements are problematic and place stress on children and carers.
- Kin carers can go to great lengths to make contact happen and take responsibility more often for supervising arrangements than is the case with non-kin carers.
- Contact may need a more differentiated response with participants being clearer about the purpose of contact.

Research shows clearly that there is a greater chance of contact with birth parents if the child is placed with extended family (F5, A24, E5). Furthermore, contact with parents is likely to be more frequent and consistent for children in kin care than for children in non-kin care (F3, F5, B17, B44, F23, F12, A24).

Continuing parental contact often benefits children's emotional and social development (D1) and provides some continuity for the child. When children live away from parents, but have frequent contact with them, the child's sense of belonging, identity, self-esteem and general well-being tend to be better (F56, E49, D12).

In the UK, Rowe et al (A24) found contact in kin placements was three times more likely than in non-kin placements; in 64 per cent of kin placements, there was contact with at least one of the child's parents. The authors suggest that, at a practical level, the fact that children were not always the focus of the visit made contact feel easier.

Richards (A22) found that of children being cared for by grandparents, almost 50% had contact with parents, 27% had contact only with the child's mother, while 10.5% had contact with the father only. Only 13% of the children had no contact with either parent (and this figure included children living with grandparents as a result of a parental death). Of the children in this study, 39% had daily contact with parents, 12% had weekly contact and 16% monthly contact.

Farmer and Moyers (A5) found children living with relatives had far more contact with their fathers (43%) compared to those placed with strangers (26%). Only 18 per cent of kin placed children had no contact with either parent, compared to 38 per cent in non-kin care. The researchers felt this may be partly due to some of them living with paternal relatives. Using semi-structured interviews, Doolan et al (A4) interviewed carers in 23 placements and found that contact with parents and extended family was happening in 19 of the placements. It was evident that caregivers made substantial efforts to ensure that contact took place. This was notable, especially as a number of the parents' lifestyles made it difficult for carers to keep contact with them.

Bergerhead (C1) reports the patterns in Sweden in kinship care that promote contact and parental involvement in the placement. She found that in kin placements:

- there tends to be more contact
- contact is often initiated by relatives as well as parents
- parents more easily join in family celebrations
- relatives arrange meetings around children
- children maintain contact with fathers as well as mothers and with both sides of the family network.

Berrick et al (F5) found that of 146 kinship placements, 81 per cent reported regular contact (compared to 58% of non-related placements); of these, 56 per cent of children saw parents at least once a month (compared to only 32% in non-kin care). Chipungu et al (B17) found that parents with children in relative placements were more likely to be in telephone contact, write or give gifts.

More recent studies are more equivocal over contact, however. Sinclair et al (E46), Quinton et al (D14) and Farmer and Moyers (A5) argue that issues of contact need a more differentiated response from social care professionals. This implies greater support, management and control over the contact process, something that is less evident in kinship care.

Sinclair et al (E46) found conflict more likely with family members (54%) compared with non-relative foster carers (16%). Indeed Laws and Broad (A13) found that '... for some families, the relationships between the carer, the child and the birth parents remain complicated and problematic'; differences of view about practical matters and parenting issues (eg, discipline) 'could create tensions'. Farmer and Moyers (A5) found there were difficulties between carers and family members in significantly more relative and friends placements (54%) than in non-kin foster care (16%). These difficulties sometimes involve verbal and physical threats to the carer and could undermine placement stability.

There are some contradictory findings, however, with some studies showing contact as being infrequent in kin placements or that parents had lost touch with the children (B14, B59). Harwin et al (A8) found a tendency, as with other placements types, for contact to reduce over time.

Contact with both parents is much less common and keeping the child in touch with both parents can be difficult. This may be so if the child is placed with a relative from one side of the family who are in conflict with the other side of the family. For example, Rowe et al (A24) found that only 21 per cent of children were having contact with both parents. Hunt and Macleod (E21) found that it was common for children to lose touch with at least one parent; the loss of maternal contact was most noticeable.

Relative carers appear to work harder at helping contact happen. They promote and maintain contact with parents and other family members (A24, F12, F31, B9). Tan (A27) found most children in kin care had regular contact with parents; for the most part, this was informally arranged by the carers. Relatives persist despite facing difficulties in managing contact (F27, F36). This is perhaps due to the fact that relatives are more likely than stranger foster carers to see themselves as responsible for organising contact (F31, F39) and for making it work; or it may be because there is little or no social work support to help make contact happen.

Farmer and Moyers (A5) found that supervised contact was supervised less by social work staff in kinship placements (27%) as opposed to non-kin placements (45%), with family members having to manage complex arrangements with sensitivity. There was evidence of contact that was detrimental to the child in more non-kin foster care placements (45%) than kin placements (31%). Contact levels with aunts, uncles and cousins also appear higher for children living with relatives and friends (A4, A1); Farmer and Moyers (A5) found it to be 55 per cent, compared to 26 per cent of children with non-kin carers.

Hunt's (E20) review implies that after court proceedings, contact tends to wither away. Where children are placed with their paternal family this may pose a barrier to contact for the maternal family side, but it did not seem to affect fathers as much when children were placed in the maternal family. Carers wanted support 'to manage the emotional turmoil' of organising or facilitating contact.

While research shows that contact is more frequent in kin care, it is not clear from the studies if that contact is associated with good outcomes for children. Contact is happening at a greater frequency and with more intensity; this can amplify both the positive and negative effects of increased parental contact for children. Contact can be, and is, difficult in a number of situations, according to the research evidence (A24, A22, A12, C6, B17). Conflict with relatives can undermine children's perspectives of their parents, or parents can damage children's perspectives of their carers. Children can get caught up in family conflicts (A12, A24, E21).

Richards (A22) discovered that grandparents were concerned about poor-quality contact and the impact it had on the child, and wanted to know where they could get help with this issue. Just over one-third of grandparents said their relationship with their own son or daughter had 'worsened' since they began to care for their grandchild.

A key concern of social workers is that kin-placed children may be more at risk because of the carers' unwillingness to enforce contact restrictions (F14). Research has shown that court-ordered contact arrangements are sometimes breached in kinship placements. Hunt and Macleod (E21) found this to be so in four of 22 cases, although only one incident resulted in an allegation of further abuse, which was unproven. Terling-Watt (B59) found seven of 19 relatives ignored or overrode the arrangements because they did not understand or believe that the parents presented a risk to the child.

findings related to outcomes: reunification, legal permanence and adoption

Key messages

- Initially, children in kinship care are slower to reunify with parents than children in non-kin placements.
- However, more recent studies suggest that levels of reunification even out over time.
- Many children gain legal permanence with relatives (most commonly residence orders) and are no longer receiving help from children's services.
- Relative caregivers do not generally favour adoption as a permanency option.
- Kin-placed children are less likely to be adopted than those in non-kin placements.
- Case plans for children in kinship care are less likely to include adoption.
- Children in kinship foster care are less likely to have legal permanence.

reunification

Until relatively recently, research suggested that children in kin care were less likely to be reunited with their birth parents (B60, B4, F7, B45, F5, F49, F58). However, more recent longitudinal studies suggest this is not the case. The longer the placement goes on, the more these differences disappear. Needell et al (F38) found that after six years, similar proportions of children from non-kin and kinship foster care were reunified with their birth parents. While kinship care may inhibit early reunification to parents, it does not seem to preclude it.

The evidence in the UK is that most children who leave public care return to their parents. Bullock et al (E8) found that 82 per cent of 450 children in substitute care had returned home to their families within five years (although sometimes only for a brief period). If a child does not return home within the first six weeks of placement, then their chance of going home early is reduced and they increasingly lose contact with family and parents. Nearly 60 per cent of all children in care go home within six weeks; 20 per cent go back within the first week (E7).

UK research is somewhat contradictory as to whether kinship care promotes or inhibits reunification. Kosenen's (A11) report on children placed with relatives showed children were more likely to return home, whereas Rowe et al (A25) found only a third returned to parents (compared to 55% of children in non-relative care). More recently, Farmer and Moyers (A5) found slightly more children returned home from unrelated foster care (28%) than from relatives (21%).

Walton et al (E52) illustrated how focused efforts could restore children to kin networks when placement with strangers was initially seen as the only alternative, and Trent (E50) showed that even those children for whom adoption was initially considered the only viable plan could be restored to parents and other relatives if efforts were made to do so.

In the US, Gleeson (B33) found that reunification was a goal in 26 per cent of kin foster placements, although workers reported that they thought they would, realistically, only achieve 10 per cent (two years on, only 4% had returned home). African-American children appear much less likely than children of other ethnic groups to be reunited with birth parents. Children in supported foster placements with kin remained there twice as long as other children (F5).

Two studies suggested very little difference in reunification rates (F5, F28). Berrick et al (F5) found that, two years on, slightly more children in non-kin care had been reunified compared with those in kinship care; but after six years, slightly more children from kinship care had returned to parents.

Timescales to reunification	2 years	4 years	6 years
Living with Non-relative placement	48%	52%	53%
Family and friends placement	45%	52%	56%

F5

While kinship care may inhibit early reunification it does seem to produce successful reunifications (B7, F8). This may say something about the preparedness of the parent or child to make reunification work after more time has passed.

Here are some possible explanations as to why reunification is slower in kinship care.

- Social workers are perhaps under less pressure to reunify children if their placement is stable.
- A number of reunifications to parents are not planned but are a response to foster care breakdown; kin care tends to be more stable.
- There is insufficient planned work, or a lack of services, to enable birth parents to take children back into their care (F3, F23).
- Reunification may lead to loss of income for the family (B8).

Adoption and permanence

Adoption and permanence is another key difference. In the UK, the rates of adoption from kinship care are much lower than the rates of adoption from non-kin foster care (A24). This may be because families in the UK would mostly opt for residence orders and social workers would see this as a good permanence option, or because kin are reluctant to remove the birth parents' responsibility.

There is also concern that kin care can be overlooked, with social workers moving to adoption with strangers before fully exploring kin networks. Ryburn (E44) showed that in half of 74 contested adoptions, no prior consideration was given to the placement of children within their wider kin networks.

Kinship care does offer a model of permanence for children, but this may not fit well with many local authorities' concept of permanency planning. Young people in the Broad et al (D2) study described a feeling of 'emotional permanence' and that they felt they belonged to somebody when living in their extended family. Kinship care placement and planning are far more likely to proceed at the pace of families and carers than at the pace of the agency, which is driven by a performance and standards agenda with tight timescales.

The situation in the US is different because the legislature seeks permanence for children earlier through adoption or transfer of legal guardianship to kin caregivers. The Adoption and Safe Families Act 1997 was introduced to limit the time children stayed in foster care. It enforced strict time-frames for permanency, so kinship adoption became an increasingly important goal in permanency planning. However, there was little published policy and procedures to guide social workers (F33).

But despite the new laws, kin and non-kin foster care differ with respect to adoption rates in the US, with those in kinship care being adopted much less frequently. This appears to be the case even when a child is placed with a carer at a very young age (B9). Berrick et al found that even with the youngest children (those taken into care before the age of one), only 11 per cent of kin-placed children had been adopted after eight years; three times as many children placed with strangers (34%) had been adopted by this stage.

Kin carers generally appear not to favour adoption (E43, F54, F5, B13). Some carers do not want to be responsible for terminating the parental rights of a relative, who is often their own child (most commonly a daughter), and argue that they are already a lifelong family to the child (F5, F53, F34).

There is some contradictory evidence, however. In a sample of 267 children with short-term and future permanency goals, Bonecutter (B11) found no difference between demonstration and control groups regarding the percentage of carers in which permanency goals were achieved through adoption, transfer of legal guardianship or reunification. And an earlier research study (F32) found that the majority of kin carers (57%) were prepared to take on a court order for the child. Gabel (B27) also found that kin and non-kin carers were equal in their willingness to adopt the child.

Gleeson (B33) examined 76 cases of children in kinship foster care and found that social workers heavily influenced what options were considered with families around permanency. They found kin caregivers did not always have the opportunity to discuss permanency options. Social workers discussed adoption in 82 per cent of cases and legal guardianship in only 51 per cent of cases. Link (B45) examined outcomes for 525 kin-placed children and found that young children were more likely to be adopted or placed for adoption; those who entered kin care at 11 years or older were more likely to be discharged to family or independent living.

In a US study, Lorkovich et al (F33) interviewed 71 kin caregivers and examined the barriers and enablers to kinship adoption (see table below).

Kinship carers' views on factors affecting decision for kinship adoption in the US

barriers	enablers
• children's problems, mental/physical health	• attachment to child
• housing problems	• adequate support systems
• carers' own health problems	• sense of entitlement for the children
• lack of trust of child welfare system	• having knowledgeable and supportive workers
• complicated adoption and court processes	• desire and belief to support adoption process
• problems with birth parents	

Chipungu et al (B17) found that care plans for children in kinship care were less likely to include adoption. They also found that 69 per cent of social workers thought that relatives believed adoption was unnecessary. Carers appeared to worry about the effect an adoption would have on their relationship with the child's birth parent. They also expressed concern about the potential complexity and expense of being drawn into the court process, particularly if the proceedings were contested.

Legal proceedings are often difficult and grandparents can feel powerless, with lawyers and social workers making decisions for them (A29).

Children in kin foster care reach legal permanence more slowly than children in non-kin foster care. Adoption levels in kin care may be shaped by the approach taken by caseworkers (F60). Indeed, the concept of specific legal 'ownership' of a child, as in adoption, is very much a white European/American notion. This differs from African, Asian and South Pacific cultures where ideas about collective responsibility for children have more currency. In South Africa, for example, the philosophy of Ubuntu (collective responsibility for children) shapes the behaviours of relatives and friends. This is captured in the saying, 'It takes a whole village to raise a child'. Families from different cultures may not share the same pre-occupations with legal ownership. In the USA, however, critics argue that permanency planning is overlooked in family and friends placements and therefore children are left in a harmful situation of 'legal limbo' (F45).

key research messages: kinship carers and birth parents

kinship carers – strengths and needs

Key messages

- The dominant profile of kinship carers is different to non-kin foster carers.
- Kin caregivers tend to be older and the majority are grandparents.
- Kinship carers commonly experience loss and significant changes in lifestyle and family relationships as a result of the placement.
- They often take on caring in an unplanned way and are usually highly committed to the child they are looking after.
- Kin caregivers are more likely to have physical and mental health problems and are more likely to be under stress than non-kin foster carers.
- A higher number of kin caregivers are lone carers compared to non-kin carers.
- Kin caregivers generally have fewer financial and material resources at their disposal and are more likely to be living in poverty or suffering financial hardship.
- They are also less likely to have formal education, training or knowledge in child development.
- Kinship carers receive less help, support, information, financial assistance and services from social care and other agencies.

carers' profile

The profile of kinship carers is different to that of non-kin foster carers. They tend to be older people, have more health needs and often have less financial resources of their own. They commonly take the care of a child unexpectedly in reaction to a crisis rather than as a planned event. A prime motivation for carers is that they often have a pre-existing relationship with a child and they do not want to see the child go into public care (B31, A4); this is a recurring theme as to why kinship care placements happen (A3, F25).

The majority of kin carers are grandparents, mostly on the maternal side of the family. In a sample of 96 carers in an English shire county, Doolan et al (A4) found that 57% were grandparents, 25% aunts and uncles, 9% step-parents and 5% friends (the rest were siblings and cousins). In the same study, a separate sample of 37 children in a London borough found that two-thirds were living with grandparents. Farmer and Moyers (A5) found that 45% of kinship carers were grandparents, 32% were uncles and aunts, and 18% were friends. Relatives or friends carers are more likely to have chronic illness or disability and to live in overcrowded conditions.

impact on carers

Kinship carers clearly 'make sacrifices and incur losses' when they take on a child's care (A5). They often have to give up work or retirement or the friendship networks they once had. They have to adjust to being carers again and have to change their lifestyles and plans. O'Brien et al (B50) surveyed a sample of 35 kinship carers and found that:

- the majority became carers without advance notice
- they felt both love towards the children and burdened by them
- obstacles encountered included a lack of information and concrete support
- all experienced change in family dynamics
- they needed help in identifying sources of support
- many felt pressured into obtaining legal orders to secure legal permanence for the child.

Grandparents often experience more psychological problems and stress than stranger foster carers. They do not have time to adjust, they have to face family crises and they lose their freedoms and future plans (C2).

US research also indicates that kinship carers are more likely to be older and are most often grandparents. There is also an implication in the literature that being older is some type of disadvantage. But while older people are more prone to poverty and illness, they also often have greater knowledge and certainly have greater experience. The idea that old age is, in itself, a disadvantage for a carer is not proven; it relies on assumptions and negative stereotyping.

A US study of over 600 kin-care homes (F51) found 83 per cent of carers thought it best that the child remained with them; in 60 per cent of cases, the child lived with a grandparent. Grandmothers felt an obligation to care for their grandchildren and many expressed surprise and disappointment at the other grandparents' refusal to help (B32). Bonecutter (B11) in the US looked at 267 children and found that 70 per cent of caregivers were single carers (widowed, divorced or never married). Of the carers surveyed, 96 per cent were African-American and 80 per cent were related to the children's birth mother (61% being the child's grandparents). Bonecutter also found that African-American grandmothers had significantly more grandchildren in their care.

Goodman et al (B34) interviewed 373 grandmothers providing informal private kin care and 208 carers awarded custody through the child welfare system (ie, public kinship foster care). The study found that formal kinship foster care was 2.7 times more likely to be used because of parental drug misuse; these kin placements were 60 per cent more likely to have happened because of parental neglect. Private kinship carers had provided care for longer and were more likely to be sharing decision making with the child's parents; a substantial proportion of these carers (40%) had also assumed care because of parental drug abuse and neglect. The findings imply that child welfare services were successful in targeting those families most at risk. However, many private kin carers have similar problems and needs. Taking on a caring role in an unplanned way was a common feature of kin care. Often this meant changes in relationships, with grandparents experiencing loss of their role as grandparent and often conflict in relations with birth parents. Farmer and Moyers (A5) found that difficulties between carers and family members occurred significantly more often in kinship care (54%) than non-kin placements (16%).

Landry-Meyer and Newman (B42) interviewed 26 grandparents in transition to becoming carers again and found three key themes:

- the unplanned nature of taking on a caregiving role
- the need for clarity of this new role
- experiencing role conflict (from grandparent to 'parent').

commitment

Kinship carers are often highly committed to the child they are looking after, in spite of the difficulties they face. Farmer and Moyers (A5) found that 65 per cent of kin carers were 'very committed', compared to just under a third (31%) of non-kin foster carers. This commitment was linked to placement stability. Kinship carers tended to treat the children they looked after like their own children and extended family appear to accept them as children of the family.

In their recent surveys of carers, Broad et al (D2), Pitcher (A21) and Richards (A22) all confirm the commitment these carers make and the joy they experience, as well as the frustrations and difficulties arising from often inadequate support services. They also talk about their social isolation and financial hardship.

difficulties

Farmer and Moyers (A5) found that relative carers appeared to be struggling to cope with the children they were looking after. This was the case with just under half (45%) of relative carers, but with less than a third (30%) of unrelated carers; the main difficulty was dealing with the child's behaviour. Helfinger, Kelly and Taylor-Richardson (B39) also found evidence of increased strain among kinship caregivers, which was comparable to that experienced by parents of a child with serious emotional disturbance.

From her survey and focus groups with Pakistani, Muslim, Sikh and Asian carers and Chinese grandparents, Richards' (A22) found little evidence, despite some assumptions to the contrary, that these carers receive additional help from the extended family. These carers tended to rely on the immediate family in times of crisis. This was difficult if there were requirements also to take responsibility for relatives who may be elderly or not living in UK.

Grandparents report finding it difficult to adapt to the physical demands of young children and hard to do the things children want to do (A22). They also find that attitudes to parenting and discipline have changed, so it is hard for them to know what is acceptable (C2).

In an Australian study, Spence (C11) noted the considerable personal cost to caregivers – financial, emotional and physical. He found high levels of stress for caregivers allied to low levels of support and monitoring of children's safety and well-being.

health needs

Kinship caregivers appear to experience more mental and physical health problems than non-kin carers. Whitley et al (B64) found that the average age of caregiver grandmothers was between 55 and 57, and many had health problems. Solomon and Marx (B58) found grandparents who were caring for more than one child tended to have poorer health. Sands and Goldberg-Glen (B54) found that older grandparents had more stress due to the loss of a spouse or ill health. And Farmer and Moyers (A5) found that twice as many relatives and friends carers had problems associated with their health and age, which affected their ability to manage the child.

In a sample of 100 African-American kin caregivers, most were found to be grandmothers. The majority were single and on benefits. Most suffered at least one ailment including diabetes, high blood pressure and obesity; indeed, 45 per cent rated their health as fair to poor. Education and intervention strategies for carers' health were seen to be important and there was a need for a greater policy and service focus on grandparent caregivers' health (B31).

Billing et al (B10) found that compared to the general population, kinship carers were more likely to have mental or physical health problems and financial problems.

Percentage of children living with caregivers with...	poor mental health	poor mental health and low income	fair or poor physical health
Children with parents	16%	25%	4%
Children with relatives	26%	33%	14%%

Cimmarusti et al (B18) looked at caregivers' burdens and social support (as perceived by kin caregivers) and measured them against emotional distress levels. In a sample of 63 caregivers who elected to take part in the study, they found that caring had a direct effect on the degree of emotional distress. The authors suggest that more attention needs to be paid to the emotional state of caregivers and that services should enhance carers' parenting abilities while respecting the social support networks that many kin caregivers already have in place.

The evidence on whether kin carers are more likely to be lone carers is mixed. The Farmer and Moyers (A5) study found the proportions in the UK were fairly similar, with lone carers representing 21 per cent of relative/friends carers and 14 per cent of non-kin foster carers. Doolan et al (A4) found that of 37 children in London boroughs, two-thirds were living with lone carers. This may be linked with ethnicity because in the US, black and minority ethnic carers are more likely to be single carers (B32).

financial pressures

A recurring theme in the research is that kinship carers have fewer financial and material resources at their disposal (B36). Sands and Goldberg-Glen (B5), in a study of 129 grandparents, found that 41 per cent of African-American grandparents were living below or on the poverty line; 58 per cent had not completed high-school education so struggled with employment.

Most kinship caregivers have less formal education than non-kin foster carers. Kin carers are also less likely to have been trained as carers and have few formal academic qualifications, with less knowledge of child development. Some studies, such as Gaudin and Sutphen (B28), have suggested that kin carers have less appropriate expectations for young children; however, even in this study, placement with kin and non-kin both fell within the 'average quality of care range'.

kin carers' skills

Harden et al (B36), in a study of 51 non-kin and 50 kin caregivers, found that after controlling for age, the two groups of caregivers showed no difference with respect to parenting attitudes. However, by contrast Fitzpatrick and Reeve (C2), in a survey of grandparents, noted that the grandparents had low energy for children's activities and lacked knowledge of modern parenting practices. Moreover, Tripp De Robertis and Litrownik (B62) looked at disciplinary practices of 70 foster parents (kin and non-kin) and examined aggression in their eight-year-old foster children. Kinship foster carers were rated as more likely than non-kin foster parents (64.8% vs 30.2%) to report using harsh discipline.

Drawing from the literature, one study attempted to identify some of the characteristics of kin caregivers that might raise practitioner concern when assessing a kin care placement:

- caregiver history of involvement with child protection services
- poor home conditions and overcrowded household
- poor parenting skills
- difficulties in working with agencies
- difficulties in working with parents (either too much conflict or an excessively permissive approach to parents when there are child protection concerns).
  B8

These findings are only a guide from their research; all checklists need to be treated with caution because they overlook the context and complexity of individual people and their situations. They can also overlook carers' strengths.

In the UK, Farmer and Moyers (A5) considered that fewer kinship carers (47%) had 'exceptional parenting skills' when compared with non-related foster carers (81%) who were selected and trained to provide high-quality care. Triseliotis et al (A28) found increasing concern about kin care in Scotland because of relatives being slow to work with social workers, the limited resources of carers and the inability of some carers to protect children from abuse within the family.

In his research review of foster care, Sinclair (D16) suggests caution:

> Attempts to provide kin care in an unreflective belief that relative care is 'better' might lead to the recruitment of some 'reluctant relatives': the present group largely volunteer themselves. This in turn might lower placement quality.

Finally, there is a range of evidence that shows kinship carers are different in that they receive less help, support, information, financial assistance and services from social care and other agencies than do non-kin foster carers (E20, D10, A4).

birth parents

Key messages

- Birth parents can have a significant impact on kinship care and are important in making and supporting the placements.
- Difficult relationships between birth parents and carers can put pressure on placements.
- Parental participation in decision making is limited, particularly for fathers.
- Mental health and substance abuse problems for parents are increasingly common (mostly in the US), leading to increased use of kin care.
- Parents have higher levels of contact with children in kinship care.
- Caregivers' perception of the birth parents co-operating with care plans and contact is associated higher rates of reunification.
- There is limited research on the role of birth parents in kinship placements.

bonds and attachments

Birth parents, like carers, have needs in their own right. Birth parents can be one of the most positive and negative influences on children and carers in kin care arrangements.

When children separate from their parents they do not easily forget them. Studies show foster children are preoccupied with their parents (E10). There are 'best practice' and legal requirements to involve parents in decision making and promote contact with their children. In most cases kin carers will at least need to consult with parents on decisions, because parents still share parental responsibility. A number of carers hope for improvements from the birth parents; grandmothers in Gibson's (B31) study (a small sample of 12) were frustrated with their own children (the parents) but hoped that the situation would improve.

support and contact

Birth parents can have a significant impact on kinship placements. Getting good co-operation appears to be important. Triseliotis (D18) identified that when carers have inclusive attitudes towards the birth family, this is one of the factors that is associated with successful placements. In the US, Testa and Shook-Slack (F50) found that when caregivers perceived that birth parents were co-operating with contact and care plans, this was associated with much higher rates of reunification to parents.

In kinship care, Johnson and Walfogel (F26) found that the most common living arrangement for children whose mother was in prison was with grandparents. Where the father was incarcerated, the most common living arrangement was with the mother or stepmother. Indeed, in the US kinship care for children who have parents in prison is rising; in particular, there are increasing numbers of black women in prison (B26).

parents' problems

Brooks and Barth (B13) found children who had been drug-exposed and placed with relatives did worse on a range of measures than children who had not been exposed to drugs. Having substance-abusing parents is one of the reasons why there are increasing numbers of children coming into public care and why numbers of kinship care placements in the US have grown. Testa et al (F51) found that in a sample of more than 600 kinship care homes, involving over 1,000 children, 60 per cent of mothers had substance abuse problems.

Jendrek (F25) interviewed 114 grandparents who provided regular care for their grandchild and found that 73% of the mothers had emotional problems, 53% had a drug problem, 48% had a mental health problem and 44% had an alcohol problem.

fathers

By contrast, the focus on fathers in kinship care is almost non-existent and little is known about them. The role of fathers was explored in a study by O'Donnell (B51). In a sample of 74 families who had a child or children in kinship care, he found:

- Social workers had little information on, or contact with, African-American fathers whose children were in kinship care.
- Social workers were more likely to identify fathers' weaknesses and lacked information about the fathers' strengths.
- Fathers whose children were in paternal kinship care saw their children more compared to those in maternal kinship care.
- The race of the social worker was not significantly related to the extent of father involvement.
- Social workers rarely felt that non-contact with the father would impede case progress.
- Many African-American fathers wished to avoid working with child welfare services because of previous bad experiences.

O'Donnell (B52) looked at birth fathers' participation and found that, in the cases of 241 children in kinship care, social workers had never contacted 68 per cent (132) of fathers and 70 per cent of fathers had never been involved in any permanency planning for their children. The study suggested that a robust policy on participation is needed if practice is to change.

service delivery issues: a framework for policy and practice

a distinct policy framework

This section examines how we might re-think the way services are organised for kinship care in light of evidence from research. The central argument is that kinship care should have its own framework for policy and practice rather than being assimilated into, or tacked onto, traditional foster care services. In the current context, kinship carers often appear to be treated as second-class foster carers.

Kinship care is different from other care arrangements supported by the state. Kin care could be seen as a distinct care type that is used as an alternative to public care, as a placement option while a child is in public care and as a permanency option for children leaving public care. The fact that kin care can span a range of alternative care placements marks it out as different.

Figure 3

where to locate policy and practice for kinship care?

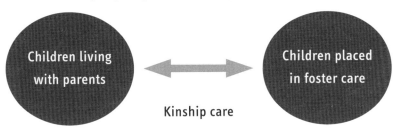

Kinship care

As we have seen, children in kin care, their carers, birth parents and families all face different and challenging issues that cannot easily be addressed by trying to fit their needs into an orthodox fostering system. Historically, fostering was designed and resourced for a different purpose: the recruitment, selection, management and retention of strangers to look after non-related children. As a consequence, it can negatively discriminate against kin care.

The axis illustrated in Figure 3 shows a polemic view of different types of placement for children. Kinship care would be located somewhere along the centre of this axis. For many children, placement with close relatives (usually grandparents, or aunts and uncles) may be much closer to the experience of living with their parents than placement with a stranger in foster care would be. Kinship placements could be located at a number of different points on the axis, depending on the nature and quality of the relationships children have with the relative caregivers and their particular circumstances. Despite the obvious different types of kin placement, the systems designed to support these carers tend also to be polarised. Either kinship carers get little of no attention and support, or they are fitted into a foster care system that was designed for non-kin carers.

It seems that the type of assessment and support for children and kinship carers needs to be more sensitive and flexible to the needs of that particular child in that particular placement. It needs to recognise that the placement could be located on a number of points on the axis depending on a range of factors. As Aldgate and McIntosh (A1) explain: '... kinship care is seen as a complex solution to serious family problems. It demands an equally sophisticated and varied response from professionals.'

information

A key difference between kin and non-kin foster carers is the way they become connected to the agency (F38). Foster carers are recruited, selected and trained in a planned way; kinship carers often emerge responding to a crisis in the child's life.

Many kinship placements happen because a family member comes forward to offer to look after the child. Farmer and Moyers (A5) found this had occurred in 86 per cent of placements; often the child was already living with a relative.

Good-quality information for kin carers is vital. Morgan (A19) found that the vast majority of local authorities (87%) do not provide written information to carers about services and support available, with only seven per cent indicating that information is available for children living in kinship care. Carers want improved information about law, benefits and entitlements, including the complaints system (A22, A21). Moreover, Richards (A22) found there were considerable barriers to Pakistani, Muslim, Sikh and Chinese grandparents accessing information and appropriate services.

A lack of information disadvantages carers who may be unaware of services and the choices available to them. Social workers tend have low levels of knowledge about kinship care and carers want more information (A4). There is also a distinct lack of support for social workers (C11); too few have policy or practice frameworks to guide them (D2). Peters (B53) analysed 50 child welfare workers' responses to training and found that while they expressed strong positive feelings about kinship care, the lack of a clear policy regarding work with kin left them feeling at risk of making an error.

Carers need information that outlines roles, responsibilities, rights, support services and financial assistance, but they find it very hard to obtain such information (A22, D2). Children also expressed a need for more information about their placements and the support available (A4).

Good-quality written information – for carers, children and birth parents – that spells out clearly the local authority's approach to kinship care is a key component of a service framework. This needs to be backed up by a supported and informed social worker to guide everyone through the process.

assessment

A new approach to assessment is needed – one that recognises the differences in kinship care. Most assessment models have been built from the assessment of orthodox foster care and, although they have been adapted for kinship care (regulation 38), they are still inadequate. Morgan (A19) found that in the UK, less than half the local authorities surveyed had specific guidelines that covered the assessment of kin care as distinct from traditional foster care.

The Department for Children, Schools and Families is now proposing that at the point of a core assessment, local authorities should ensure, when assessing the wider family and environmental factors, that 'consideration is given to the willingness and capacity of the wider family to care for the child on a shorter or longer-term basis'. This proposal is set out in the White Paper *Care Matters* (H7).

In practice, kinship carers experience a range of assessment approaches. Some caregivers are not sure if they have been formally assessed at all, while others describe a lengthy and detailed process that included medicals and wider family interviews. Many families find social work assessment intrusive and demeaning, and dominated by a risk orientation. Doolan et al (A4) found caregivers were critical of the time devoted to focusing on risk when contrasted with the energy devoted to understating their needs. Pitcher (A21) found grandparents expected to be assessed and 'checked out' but they wanted this to be done in a respectful way that recognised their skills and the differences between them and the worker. Farmer and Moyers (A5) found a number of kin carers felt the assessment approach for stranger foster carers did not reflect their needs well.

The dominant profile of kin caregivers is different. The advantages and strengths of these placements are not helped by standard fostering assessments. A unique assessment and approval process is required – not one that tolerates lower expectations of care, but one that reflects the different nature of the costs and benefits of kinship care. For example, as we have seen, the quality of the relationships between child and carers and between carers and birth parents are key to successful placements. This quality of relationship and commitment needs to be balanced against, for example, caregivers perhaps having less formal knowledge of child development. In addition, the views of the wider family could be more involved in assessing placements. None of this information is available when assessing stranger foster carers.

Kin caregivers need to be assessed to care for a member of their family who, in many case, they are already caring for. In two-thirds (65%) of placements with kin, the suitability of the carers was assessed when the child was already living with them (A5). Carers feel assessment should be more a joint examination of the needs of the child and their own needs for support and assistance in providing safe and healthy care.

A key distinction, then, in the assessment for kinship care is that social workers are assessing the viability of the placement (which is often already made), whereas the focus of orthodox fostering assessments is the attitudes, resources and skills of the carers.

Kinship care assessments could be based on collaborative models of assessment as a practice social workers do with families, rather than do to them. In this way, carers and social workers can work together to construct a profile of the child and carers' needs, taking a whole-family approach. This may not be an orthodox procedural or expert professional model of assessment, but it does place greater emphasis on professional engagement with a range of stakeholders, and the context in which the child is growing up. This exchange and action model of assessment (G14) builds on the skills and knowledge of the family as well as professionals.

Professional attitudes need addressing through training and debate so that practitioners can become more aware of the strengths and limitations of this care type. Research shows that in most kin placements, the majority of social workers (57%) had initially not considered this as an option (A5). It should be remembered that assessments have predictive limitations; for example, Rowe et al (A24) found little difference in successful outcomes for children between those kin placements that followed a full agency assessment and those that had already been made without any assessment having taken place.

planning and decision making

Kinship placements are often made quickly, as reaction to a crisis, with care planning happening after placements are made. It seems essential, therefore, to involve children and families in decision making. However, social workers report practical, ideological and organisational barriers to involving families (A4). In practice, practitioners are used to working with decision-making models that, conceptually and physically, are dominated by professionals. Family Group Conferences (FGCs) are one effective way of changing this by bringing families together to make shared plans for children. The systematic application of FGCs would ensure that families are fully involved in decision making and that possible kin placements are not overlooked. The FGC would enable families and professionals to collaborate, organise appropriate supports and decide how to deal with any issues of conflict.

The way kin placements are approved needs attention. The development of kinship care panels, with their own unique process and body of knowledge, could be used to agree supported placements. Panels could consist of both professionals and carers to monitor the quality of assessments and ensure that supports and payments are implemented and systematically reviewed.

A distinct kinship care budget would support decision making on the approval process that ensures payments to kin carers are committed, at rates equivalent to fostering rates (see the section on 'financial support' below). In addition, financial support might include assisted legal costs for section 8 orders, housing or payments to carers to purchase specific practical help or services.

Kinship care panels could make links to local carers' networks and help provide advice, information and support to professionals, carers, children, parents and other agencies working with these placements.

financial support

The importance of having the right financial support in place for kinship care cannot be overstated.

We have seen that relative carers make enormous sacrifices to look after children and often suffer financial hardship. The level of financial support offered to help kin carers varies widely and often appears unfair. Link (B45) questions the logic of strangers being paid more than relatives to look after children, and grandparents being paid more than parents receive on state benefits, to look after their grandchild.

At the outset of the arrangement and thereafter, most families need detailed advice about the financial supports available, the benefit and tax consequences, and the local authority's powers. Some families need capital finance, especially at the beginning of an unplanned placement, some need revenue payments and others need both.

When children arrive in an emergency, carers often need practical support and finance to get beds and bed linen, clothes and other necessities for the children. A Social Fund loan is not sufficient. However, there is a wide disparity and inconsistency in decisions about financial payments in apparently similar cases, even within the same local authorities (G16).

There is a common ideological belief that families should not receive income for caring for 'their own' children. Indeed, there are some legislative examples of this manner of thinking. The Carers and Disabled Children Act 2000 specifically prohibits payments to family, and the Children (Leaving Care) Act 2000 also provides for less support for children leaving the care of relatives.

A system of financial assistance is needed that realistically meets the expenses of caring for children who may have otherwise been in public care. However, when children are placed with relatives in emergency situations, carers often find their bargaining position severely weakened by the fact that the children are already with them before any support package can be negotiated (D2, A4).

A clear policy framework for the reimbursement of kinship care is required (D15). The Munby judgement (R (L and Others) V Manchester City Council 2002 (H4)) now requires that kin carers who are approved as foster parents under the same provisions are to have the same financial entitlement. However, it appears that kin are often considered second-class foster carers; local authorities may be reluctant to invest in a group of caregivers who are unlikely to care for other children or become an ongoing agency resource (D10).

It may be that a differentiated model of payment for carers could be developed, providing different levels of support based on an assessment of need. This could still provide a baseline amount of minimum allowances for all kin carers, but would also ensure that a greater amount of resources are dedicated and committed to those most in need. Providing baseline national allowances through tax benefits or national child benefit or child allowance provision in the form of a state entitlement, such as an unsupported child allowance as in New Zealand (A4), would ensure an entitlement for all carers and that resources follow children. Where the agency becomes involved in making or supporting the child's placement and the child's needs warrant it, this could then be augmented by social care agency resources and payments.

A more progressive child-care policy would perhaps enable the same amount of resources to be committed to keeping a child out of the public care system as is used to keep them in that system. Such a policy would send a clear message that the use of kinship care is at least as important as other state care options. It would also need to ensure that there are no financial disincentives for carers to move children to legally permanent solutions if these placements continued to require a high level of financial support to be effective.

All parties need clear guidance on the issue of financial support and this would be a critical component of a comprehensive policy framework

social work and support services

Most children in kinship foster care are treated unequally by child welfare services (B7, C11). Evidence from research suggests that despite similarities in the children being looked after (F41), kinship foster carers receive less support, training and finance, as well as fewer services (F5).

Kin care placements are visited less frequently by social workers than non-kin foster carers (B29, A5). In one study, more than a quarter of kinship foster carers had had no contact with a caseworker within the previous year (B20). Indeed, relatives who take a residence order often get no social work support at all. Farmer and Moyers found kin placements were significantly more likely to sustain if an allocated social worker was provided and continued to work with the placement.

Social workers can make false and racist assumptions about there being additional family support in black and minority ethnic communities (D9). They must be careful not to make assumptions about family networks; they must also recognise that agencies have underdeveloped services for black and minority ethnic groups.

O'Brien (C5) found that kinship carers often misunderstood the reasons for social work involvement and could not distinguish between social work support and supervision. Families saw the agency in a monitoring role and so lower levels of contact with social workers, after assessment, was welcomed because carers felt it meant they had approval and would keep the child. Families also often believed they had to manage independently, not knowing what help and support they could call on.

Kin caregivers also express the need for social work support for themselves to help them deal with family dynamics and contact issues, and to strengthen child development knowledge and behaviour management. When assistance is called upon, kin carers most frequently request help in obtaining legal assistance and financial support (A15), respite care (F5, B48), and training and support groups (F57).

Grandparents report that when they take on the care of a child in a family crisis, their relationship with the parents gets worse (A22). In kinship care inter-family and intra-family relationships can be more complicated and can create stress for carers. So good practice would require an awareness of family networks, family systems and the use of systemic interventions to help kin families (E37).

New kinship carers will often need intervention and support around issues of loss, separation, divided loyalties, changes in roles, managing contact and conflict with birth parents. Grandparents face dealing with loss, changing family relationships (because of their new role as primary carer) and responding to their grandchildren's insecurity (F43). This can require skilled interventions from social workers (see F10 for a useful guide to practice interventions). However, Peters (B53) found that social workers were negative about the greater time needed to work with kinship foster care placements and had concerns in dealing with triangulation between carers, birth parents and themselves.

Recent studies have highlighted a range of support services that carers find useful. However, they have also identified carers' concerns that services evaporate after an initial settling-in period and that carers are frequently not assessed as having needs in their own right. These are some recent findings.

- Carers valued the support of social workers, and young people spoke highly of individual social workers who gave practical advice and support (D2, A9).
- Carers have needs in their own right, including health and emotional support (A22, B42, B31).
- Grandparents value support groups and say it makes a positive difference to their lives (A21, A22).
- Where a residence order was made after an intervention by

children's services, cases tended to be closed shortly thereafter – and carers then found it difficult to access support services (A22, A9).

- Generally, social work support tended to tail off to very little after the initial support (A22, D2).

- Children want an ongoing supportive relationship with the same social worker, but this is not common (A4).

- Short breaks that enable the carer to have some rest were seen as a very practical and much needed support in some cases (A4, A5).

Support services for kinship care should adopt an ecological, systemic and collaborative model of social work, seeking to engage the whole family and the child's networks. In orthodox foster care, the accepted practice is that social work support is split between the child and caregiver. This historical pattern arose out of the needs of foster carers for their own recruitment and retention, so when the child moves the family placement worker does not go with them but stays with the carer. Services will need to decide if they develop specialist kinship placement workers to ensure support for carers, or if they continue to draw upon the usual family placement resources.

New approaches to kinship care will require training in developing skills of working with whole family systems and forging agreements with wider supportive networks of families and other agencies. A key task will be negotiating partnerships with other service-providers to enable specialist support – counselling, practical assistance in the home, housing, support groups for carers, specialist behaviour advice, and so on. This requires a social worker to work with a wide range of people within families' networks. There will also be requirements for cultural and cross-generational competencies to be effective (E37).

O'Brien (C6) identifies from research the optimal components needed to maintain a co-operative network of relationships in kinship care. These are goals that the agency and family members must work towards together. The optimal aspirations are (see Figure 4):

- Family members feel supported and respected by each other and the agency.

- The agency is satisfied that the child is adequately protected and the care arrangement is built on the principle of normalisation.

- The child is content to live in an environment free from conflict between adults, where they are loved and cared for.

Morgan (A19) found that only 15 per cent (8) of local authorities said they provided training on the use of kinship placements for children, and only 11 per cent (6) provided specific training for the potential support needs of kin carers. To compound this problem, there is a dearth of training materials for social workers and carers on family and friends care (G16). However, the National Foster Care Association (now known as Fostering Network) developed training materials for practitioners and carers to support kinship care (G9).

There is a need for innovation and new services. For example, Strozier et al (F47) studied 46 carers using a computer-based training programme over an eight-week training course. The intervention was judged as helpful in increasing caregiver skills, enhancing social support networks and building common ground between children and carers.

Figure 4:

Optimal features required for a network based on partnership

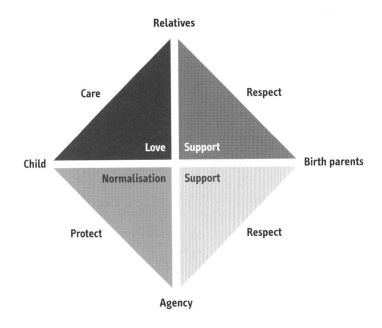

C6

multiagency work

Good interagency work is likely to be critical to the success of kin care placements and the Children Act 2004 places emphasis on partnerships. As the research shows, many children, carers and birth parents face significant health, social, behavioural, financial, housing and educational issues. And for grandparents, the demands on their time and the stress of being a caregiver (often in complex situations) compromise their ability to focus on maintaining their own physical and mental heath (F43).

Children placed with kin carers have a range of health needs – both physical and emotional – at the time they are placed; for some children, these needs may be enduring. But carers find it difficult to access the necessary health supports, especially if children's services were not directly involved. This has been found to be an issue for black and minority ethnic carers in particular, who tend to be older than white carers (A22, A13).

Birth parents, who typically have a lot of involvement in kinship placements, have been shown to have high levels of drug, alcohol and mental health problems. This means that services for them are vital if they are to take a positive role in supporting the placements through contact, short beaks and decision making.

Carers often complain that adult service workers (eg, from mental health and drug or alcohol services) are reluctant to talk to them because of client confidentiality. But grandparent carers in particular need information on how to manage if a parent comes to visit in an intoxicated or florid state (A4). Adult services and children's services will have to work better together.

In education, there are extra financial costs for carers with children attending new schools. Richards (A22) found that where children had special education needs, it was often very difficult for carers to access the necessary services. The financial costs of education extras (eg, uniform and school trips) were also difficult to meet (A13). Language barriers excluded some carers from communicating with school staff and grandparents wanted help with homework issues and computer skills.

Carers and young people really appreciated social work support in resolving education issues (A13). Carers' relationships with the school was an important part of the support network.

review and evaluation

In the research, children and carers lament the tailing off of support. It is important that plans and services are thoroughly reviewed at least on an annual basis and that services continue to target needs. Family Group Conferences are an excellent means of bringing family networks together in such a way that information is openly shared within families and between families and professionals. This model helps to keep professionals and families accountable for children and can be used to manage conflict.

Evaluation of kin care services could be done using models of research that are congruent with the values and principles of the service. Empowering models of evaluation could be used to test the effectiveness of any new services developed. Holland et al (F22) conducted an evaluation involving UK social work managers and found a culture of innovation in voluntary and statutory sectors, but with little evaluation of the effects of new interventions.

There is a need to keep building research into practice and policy developments. We need to learn more about this placement type and its effects on children and their families.

conclusion

Kinship care is on the increase and yet we are only beginning to understand its impact on the lives of some of our most vulnerable children. There is, as we have seen here, a growing body of evidence about how this type of placement affects children and their families and how state agencies and social workers are trying to work with them. On closer inspection, it is clear that these placements can produce a wide range of needs – financial and housing needs, practical equipment, as well as emotional, therapeutic and practical support. The implication is that a range of stakeholders and agencies must work together to help make kinship care work.

There are to date very few studies on kinship care that track longitudinal changes over time or set out to compare different types of kinship care. There is a real lack of studies reporting on children's views of kinship care or upon the types of services that have been effective in making kin care work. These are certainly areas for future development.

suggestions for future research

While the research and knowledge base on kinship care is growing, it is important that we continue to focus on outcomes for children and what we mean by good outcomes, from a variety of perspectives, especially the child's (B1). This may mean involving children and families more in the design of research and its implementation, analysis and dissemination.

Gleeson and Hairston (F17) propose a framework for future research to include:

- understanding experiences across cultures and in various kinship networks
- exploring sources of caregiver burden
- parents' roles before and after kinship placement
- the child's perspective on safety, permanence and well-being
- testing new models of casework service and kinship care services
- the effects of financial strategies on kinship care placements.

The quality of relationship between child and carer appears to be a key area in making placements work. Further exploration of this subject might help our understanding of why some placements endure and some do not. Critically, more research is needed on outcomes for children, particularly in relation to different types of kinship placement. Are there types of kin care that work better than others? What do longitudinal studies say about what happens to children over time? What would be the prevailing features of successful and unsuccessful placements? Do legal orders help produce better outcomes? What type of placement support works best over time?

Research into kinship care needs substantial investment; the amount of research to date is scant compared to that undertaken on residential care or adoption placements, which involve broadly similar numbers of children in state care.

Longitudinal studies from a child perspective are rare and could give us a real insight into what kinship care means for children. It would also be interesting to develop new research methodologies in which children were involved in the focus and design, analysis and dissemination of studies.

The way in which kin carers are identified and assessed is important and research shows that families most often make these placements themselves. Moreover, once a kin placement is made, placement changes are more likely to remain within the family network – and vice versa for children placed with non-kin. It appears that the early stages of intervention, involvement and decision making by the family network and formal state agencies have a defining effect on the care route the child takes and have implications for practice.

Discovering the right conditions for good kinship care practice, and identifying the social work skills and behaviours needed to help make these placements work, justifies further exploration – as do cross-cultural studies and transnational studies on policy and practice innovations with kinship care, perhaps in particular the role of Family Group Conferences in making kin placements.

Birth parents have a significant impact on the way placements come about, on planning and decision making within placements, and on how placements are supported and worked with. This requires further attention – not least because this is an area where more work could be done to help families in conflict.

The arrival of the new White paper Care Matters: Time for change will bring a fresh impetus to authorities in developing services and practice on kinship care; no doubt new services and practice innovations will emerge.

The growing number of studies, some of which have been cited here, need to have a bigger impact on policy, training, services and practice. These studies remind us that, fundamentally, children and carers are themselves usually the best judge of what works best for them. We need to work in a way that respects and values that fact

references - classified

A UK publications based on primary research on kinship care

B U.S publications based on primary research on kinship care

C Other publications from abroad (outside UK and U.S) based on primary research on kinship care

D UK publications based on secondary research, including research and literature reviews

E UK related primary research on children and their families, social work and foster care

F Publications based on secondary research from U.S. and other countries

G General political, theoretical work and training materials

H Government law, policy documents and guidance

A1
Aldgate J and McIntosh M (2006) *Looking After the Family: A study of children looked after in kinship care in Scotland.* Edinburgh: Social Work Inspection Agency

A2
Berridge D and Cleaver H (1987) *Foster Home Breakdown.* Oxford: Blackwell

A3
Broad B, Hayes R and Rushforth C (2001) *Kith and Kin: Kinship care for vulnerable young people.* London: National Children's Bureau, Joseph Rowntree Foundation

A4
Doolan M, Nixon P and Lawrence P (2004) *Growing Up in the Care of Relatives or Friends: Delivering best practice for children in family and friends care.* London: Family Rights Group

A5
Farmer R and Moyers S (2005) *Children Placed with Relatives and Friends: Placement patterns and outcomes.* (Report to the DfES) Bristol: School for Policy Studies, University of Bristol

A6
Ferguson N, Douglas G, Lowe N, Murch M and Robinson M (2004) *Grandparenting in Divorced Families.* Bristol: The Policy Press

A7
Grandparents Federation (1996) *Residence Order Allowance Survey.* Harlow: Grandparents Federation

A8
Harwin J, Owen M, Locke R and Forrester D (2001) *Making Care Orders Work: A study of care plans and their implementation.* London: The Stationery Office

A9
Hunt J (2001) 'Kinship Care, Child Protection and the Courts' in Broad B (ed), *Kinship Care: The placement choice for children and young people.* Lyme Regis: Russell House Publishing

A10
Kosonen M (1996) 'Maintaining Sibling Relationships – Neglected dimension in child care practice' *British Journal of Social Work* 26 (6)

A11
Kosonen M (1999) 'Core and Kin Siblings: Foster children's changing families' in Mullender A (ed), *We Are Family: Sibling relationships in placement and beyond*. Nottingham: BAAF

A12
Laws S (2001) 'Looking After Children within the Extended Family: Carers' views' in Broad B (ed), *Kinship Care: The placement choice for children and young people*. Lyme Regis: Russell House Publishing

A13
Laws S and Broad B (2000) *Looking After Children within the Extended Family: Carers' views*. Leicester: Centre for Social Action, De Montfort University

A14
McGlone F, Park A and Smith K (1998) *Families and Kinship*. London: Family Policy Studies Centre

A15
McLean B and Thomas R (1996) 'Informal and Formal Kinship Care Populations: A study in contrasts' *Child Welfare* 75 (5)

A16
Marsh P and Peel M (1999) *Leaving Care in Partnership*. Norwich: The Stationery Office

A17
Millham S, Bullock R, Hoise K and Hack M (1986) *Lost in Care*. Aldershot: Gower

A18
Mooney A, Statham J, with Simon A (2002) *The Pivot Generation: Informal care and work after 50*. Bristol: The Policy Press, for the Joseph Rowntree Foundation

A19
Morgan A (2003) *Survey of Local Authorities in England: Policy and practice in family and friends care*. London: Family Rights Group

A20
Philpot T (2001) *A Very Private Practice. An investigation into private fostering*. London: BAAF

A21
Pitcher D (2001) 'Assessing Grandparent Carers: A framework' in Broad B (ed), *Kinship Care: The placement choice for children and young people*. Lyme Regis: Russell House Publishing

A22
Richards A (2001) *Second Time Around: A survey of grandparents raising their grandchildren*. London: Family Rights Group

A23
Rodgers-Farmer AY (1999) 'Parenting Stress, Depression and Parenting in Grandmothers Raising their Grandchildren' *Children and Youth Services Review* 21 (5)

A24
Rowe J, Cain H, Hundleby M and Keane A (1984) *Long-term Foster Care*. London: Batsford

A25
Rowe J, Hundleby M and Garnett L (1989) *Child Care Now: A survey of placement patterns.* (Research Series 6) London: BAAF

A26
Scottish Executive (2005) *Statistics Publication Notice – Health and Care Series: Children's Social Work Statistics 2004-05 (ISSN 1479-7569).* Scottish Executive National Statistics. Online version available at www.scotland.gov.uk/Publications/2005/10/2791127/11278

A27
Tan S (2000) *Friends and Relative Care: The neglected carers.* (Unpublished dissertation for the PQ Award in Social Work.) Brunel University

A28
Triseliotis J, Borland M and Hill M (1999) *Delivering Foster Care.* London: BAAF

A29
Tunnard J and Thoburn J (1997) *The Grandparents' Supporters Project: An independent evaluation.* Harlow: Grandparents Federation

A30
Young M and Willmott P (1962) *Family and Kinship in East London.* London: Pelican

B1
Altshuler SJ and Gleeson JP (1999) 'Completing the Evaluation Triangle for the Next Century: Measuring child "well-being" in family foster care' *Child Welfare* 78 (1)

B2
Beeman S and Boisen L (1999) 'Child Welfare Professionals' Attitudes Towards Kinship Foster Care' *Child Welfare* 78 (3)

B3
Beeman S, Wattenberg E, Boisen L and Bullerdick S (1996) *Kinship Foster Care in Minnesota.* Minnesota: Center for Advanced Studies in Child Welfare, University of Minnesota School of Social Work

B4
Benedict M and White R (1991) 'Factors Associated with Foster Care Length of Stay' *Child Welfare* 70 (1)

B5
Benedict M, Zuravin S and Stallings R (1996) 'Adult Functioning of Children Who Lived in Kin Versus Non-relative Family Foster Homes' *Child Welfare* 75 (5)

B6
Berrick JD (1997) 'Assessing the Quality of Care in Kinship and Foster Family Care' *Family Relations* 46 (3)

B7
Berrick JD (1998) 'When Children Cannot Remain Home: Foster family care and kinship care' *The Future of Children: Protecting Children from Abuse and Neglect* 8 (1)

B8
Berrick JD and Needell B (1999) 'Recent Trends in Kinship Care: Public policy, payments and outcomes for children' in Curtis PA and Grady D (eds), *The Foster Care Crisis: Translating research into policy and practice.* Lincoln, NB: Child Welfare League of America and University of Nebraska Press

B9

Berrick JD, Needell B and Barth RP (1998) 'Kin as a Family and Child Welfare Resource: The child welfare worker's perspective' in Hegar RL and Scannapieco M (eds), *Kinship Foster Care: Policy, practice and research*. New York: Oxford University Press

B10

Billing A, Ehrle J and Kortenkamp K (2002) *Children Cared for by Relatives: What do we know about their well-being? (No. B-46 in the series, New Federalism: National survey of America's families.)* Washington DC: The Urban Institute. Online version available at www.urban.org/url.cfm?ID=310486

B11

Bonecutter FJ (1999) 'Defining Best Practice in Kinship Care through Research and Demonstration' in Gleeson JP and Hairston CF (eds), *Kinship Care: Improving practice through research*. Washington DC: Child Welfare League of America

B12

Brooks D (1999) 'Kinship Care and Substance-exposed Children' *The Source* (Biannual magazine of The National Abandoned Infants Assistance Resource Center) 9 (1)

B13

Brooks D and Barth R (1998) 'Characteristics and Outcomes of Drug-exposed and Non-drug-exposed Children in Kinship and Non-relative Foster Care' *Children and Youth Services Review* 20 (6)

B14

Burnette D (1999) 'Social Relationships of Latino Grandparent Caregivers: A role theory perspective' *The Gerontologist* 39 (1)

B15

Carpenter S and Clyman R (2004) 'The Long-term Emotional and Physical Well-being of Women Who Have Lived in Kinship Care' *Children and Youth Services Review* 26 (7)

B16

Chalfie D (1994) *Going It Alone: A closer look at grandparents parenting children*. Washington DC: American Association of Retired Persons

B17

Chipungu SS, Everett JE, Verdieck MJ and Jones J (1998) *Children Placed in Foster Care with Relatives: A multi-state study*. Washington DC: US Department of Health and Human Services

B18

Cimmarusti R, Derezotes DM, Skolec J and Dannenbring-Carlson D (2000) *Kinship Caregiver Burden*. Urbana-Champaign, IL: Children and Family Research Center, School of Social Work, University of Illinois at Urbana-Champaign

B19

Cook R and Ciarico J (1998) *Analysis of Kinship Care Data from the US DHHS 20National Study of Protective, Preventive and Reunification Services Delivered to Children and their Families*. (Unpublished.) US Department of Health and Human Services

B20
Dubowitz H (1990) *The Physical and Mental Health and Educational Status of Children Placed with Relatives: Final report.* Baltimore, MD: University of Maryland Medical School

B21
Dubowitz H, Feigelman S, Harrington D, Starr T, Zuravin S and Sawyer R (1994) 'Children in Kinship Care: How do they fare?' *Children and Youth Services Review* 16 (1-2)

B22
Dubowitz H, Zuravin S, Starr R, Feigelman S and Harrington D (1993) 'Behavioural Problems of Children in Kinship Care' *Journal of Behavioural and Developmental Paediatrics* 14 (6)

B23
Ehrle J, Green R and Clark R (2001) *Children Cared for by Relatives: Who are they and how are they faring?* (No. B-28 in the series, *New Federalism: National survey of America's families.*) Washington DC: The Urban Institute. Online version available at www.urban.org/url.cfm?ID=310270

B24
Ehrle J and Kortenkamp K (2002) *The Well-being of Children Involved with the Child Welfare System: A national overview.* (No. B-43 in the series, *New Federalism: National survey of America's families.*) Washington DC: The Urban Institute. Online version available at www.urban.org/url.cfm?ID=310413

B25
Fein E, Maluccio A, Hamilton J and Ward D (1983) 'After Foster Care: Outcomes of permanence planning for children' *Child Welfare* 62 (6)

B26
Fuller-Thomson E (2000) 'African American Grandparents Raising Grandchildren: A national profile of demographic and health characteristics' *Health & Social Work* 25 (2)

B27
Gabel G (1992) *Preliminary Report on Kinship Foster Family Profile.* New York: Human Resources Administration, Child Welfare Administration

B28
Gaudin J and Sutphen R (1993) 'Foster Care vs. Extended Family Care for Children of Incarcerated Mothers' *Journal of Offender Rehabilitation* 19 (3-4)

B29
Gebel T (1996) 'Kinship Care and Non-relative Family Foster Care: A comparison of caregiver attributes and attitudes' *Child Welfare* 75 (1)

B30
Gennaro S, York R and Dunphy P (1998) 'Vulnerable Infants: Kinship care and health' *Pediatric Nursing* 24 (2)

B31
Gibson PA (2002a) 'Caregiving Role Affects Family Relationships of African American Grandmothers as New Mothers Again: A phenomenological perspective' *Journal of Marital and Family Therapy* 28 (3)

B32
Gibson PA (2002b) 'African American Grandmothers as Caregivers: Answering the call to help their grandchildren' *Families in Society* 83 (1)

B33
Gleeson JP (1999a) 'Who Decides? Predicting caseworkers' adoption and guardianship discussions with kinship caregivers' in Gleeson JP and Hairston CF (eds), *Kinship Care: Improving practice through research*. Washington DC: Child Welfare League of America

B34
Goodman C, Potts M, Pasztor E and Scorzo D (2004) 'Grandmothers As Kinship Caregivers: Private arrangements compared to public child welfare oversight' *Children and Youth Services Review* 26 (3)

B35
Harden AW, Clark RL and Maguire K (1997) *Informal and Formal Kinship Care*. Washington DC: US Department of Health and Human Services

B36
Harden B, Clyman R, Kriebel D and Lyons M (2004) 'Kith and Kin Care: Parental attitudes and resources of foster and relative caregivers' *Children and Youth Services Review* 26 (7)

B37
Hatmaker C (1999) *Project REFRESH: Research and evaluation of foster children's reception into environmentally supportive homes. Final qualitative report*. Oregon: Family Policy Program, Oregon State University

B38
Hegar RL (1993) 'Assessing Attachment, Permanence and Kinship in Choosing Permanent Homes' *Child Welfare* 72 (4)

B39
Heflinger C, Kelly D and Taylor-Richardson K (2004) 'Caregiver Strain in Families of Children with Serious Emotional Disturbance: Does relationship to child make a difference?' *Journal of Family Social Work* 8 (1)

B40
Henry J (1999) 'Permanency Outcomes in Legal Guardianships of Abused/Neglected Children' *Families in Society* 80 (6)

B41
James S (2004) 'Why Do Foster Care Placements Disrupt? An investigation of reasons for placement change in foster care' *Social Service Review* 78 (4)

B42
Landry-Meyer L and Newman B (2004) 'An Exploration of the Grandparent Caregiver Role' *Journal of Family Issues* 25 (8)

B43
Le Prohn NS (1993) *Relative Foster Parents: Role perceptions, motivation and agency satisfaction*. (PhD dissertation, University of Washington, Seattle) cited in General Accounting Office (1999) *Foster Care: Kinship care quality and permanency issues*. Washington DC: General Accounting Office

B44
Le Prohn NS and Pecora P (1994) *The Casey Foster Parent Study – Research summary*. Seattle, WA: Casey Family Program

B45
Link M (1996) 'Permanency Outcomes in Kinship Care: A study of children placed in kinship care in Erie County, New York' *Child Welfare* 75 (5)

B46
Main R, Ehrle Macomber J and Green R (2006) *Trends in Service Receipt: Children in kinship care gaining ground.* (No. B-68 in the series, *New Federalism: National survey of America's families.*) Washington DC: The Urban Institute
Online version available at www.urban.org/url.cfm?ID=311310

B47
Mayfield J, Pennucci A and Lyon C (2002) *Kinship Care in Washington State: Prevalence, policy and needs.* Olympia, WA: Washington State Institute for Public Policy.
Online version available at www.wsipp.wa.gov/pub.asp?docid=02-06-3901

B48
Minkler M and Roe K (1993) *Grandmothers As Caregivers.* Newbury Park, CA: Sage

B49
Nixon P, Burford G and Quinn A (with Edelbaum J) (2005) *A Survey of International Practices, Policy and Research on Family Group Conferencing and Related Practices.* Englewood, CO: American Humane Association, National Center on Family Group Decision Making

B50
O'Brien P, Massat CR and Gleeson JP (2001) 'Upping the Ante: Relative caregivers' perceptions of changes in child welfare policies' *Child Welfare* 80 (6)

B51
O'Donnell JM (1999) 'Involvement of African American Fathers in Kinship Foster Care Services' *Social Work* 44 (5)

B52
O'Donnell JM (2001) 'Paternal Involvement in Kinship Foster Care Services in One Father and Multiple Father Families' *Child Welfare* 80 (4)

B53
Peters J (2005) 'True Ambivalence: Child welfare workers' thoughts, feelings and beliefs about kinship foster care' *Children and Youth Services Review* 27 (6)

B54
Sands RG and Goldberg-Glen RS (2000) 'Factors Associated with Stress among Grandparents Raising their Grandchildren' *Family Relations* 49 (1)

B55
Sawyer RJ and Dubowitz H (1994) 'School Performance of Children in Kinship Care' *Child Abuse & Neglect* 18 (7)

B56
Scannapieco M, Hegar R and McAlpine C (1997) 'Kinship Care and Foster Care: A comparison of characteristics and outcomes' *Families in Society* 78 (5)

B57
Shlonsky AR and Berrick JD (2001) 'Assessing and Promoting Quality in Kin and Non-kin Foster Care' *Social Service Review* 75 (1)

B58
Solomon JC and Marx J (1995) 'To Grandmother's House We Go – Health and school adjustment of children raised solely by grandparents' *The Gerontologist* 35 (3)

B59
Terling-Watt T (2001) 'Permanency in Kinship Care: An exploration of disruption rates and factors associated with placement disruption' *Children and Youth Services Review* 23 (2)

B60
Testa MF (1992) 'Conditions of Risk for Substitute Care' *Children and Youth Services Review* 14 (1-2)

B61
Timmer S, Sedlar G and Urquiza A (2004) 'Challenging Children in Kin Versus Non-kin Foster Care Perceived Costs and Benefits to Caregivers' *Child Maltreatment* 9 (3)

B62
Tripp De Robertis M and Litrownik AJ (2004) 'The Experience of Foster Care: Relationship between foster parent disciplinary approaches and aggression in a sample of young foster children' *Child Maltreatment* 9 (1)

B63
Webster D, Barth RP and Needell B (2000) 'Placement Stability for Children in Out-of-home Care: A longitudinal analysis' *Child Welfare* 79 (5)

B64
Whitley DM, Kelley SJ and Sipe TA (2001) 'Grandmothers Raising Grandchildren: Are they at increased risk of health problems?' *Health & Social Work* 26 (2)

B65
Wilson L (1996) *The 1995 Annual Client Evaluation*. Tulsa, OK: Wilson Resources

C1
Bergerhed E (1995) 'Kinship and Network Care in Sweden' in Thelen H (ed), *Foster Children in a Changing World: Documentation of the 1994 European IFCO conference in Berlin*. Berlin: Arbeitskreis Zur Forderung Von Pflegekindern E.V.

C2
Fitzpatrick M and Reeve P (2003) 'Grandparents Raising Grandchildren: A new class of disadvantaged Australians' *Family Matters* No. 66 Spring/Summer

C3
Hannah L and Pitman S (2000) *Oz Child's Kith and Kin Program*. Melbourne: Oz Child

C4
Maxwell GM and Robertson JP (1991) 'Statistics on the First Year of the Children, Young Persons and their Families Act 1989' in Maxwell GM (ed) *An Appraisal of the First Year of the Children, Young Persons and their Families Act 1989*. Wellington, New Zealand: Office of the Commissioner for Children

C5
O'Brien V (1999) 'Evolving Networks of Relative Care: Some findings from an Irish study' in Greeff R (ed), *Fostering Kinship: An international perspective on kinship foster care*. Ashgate: Aldershot

C6

O'Brien V (2001) 'Contributions from an Irish Study: Understanding and managing relative care' in Broad B (ed), *Kinship Care: The placement choice for children and young people*. Lyme Regis: Russell House Publishing

C7

Pemberton D (1999) 'Fostering in a Minority Community – Travellers in Ireland' in Greeff R (ed), *Fostering Kinship: An international perspective on kinship foster care*. Aldershot: Ashgate

C8

Portengen R and van der Neut B (1999) 'Assessing Family Strengths – A family systems approach' in Greeff R (ed), *Fostering Kinship: An international perspective on kinship foster care*. Aldershot: Ashgate

C9

Sallnas M, Vinnerljung B and Westermark PK (2004) 'Breakdown of Teenage Placements in Swedish Foster and Residential Care' *Child & Family Social Work* 9 (2)

C10

Smith AB, Gollop MM, Taylor NJ and Atwool NR (1999) Children in Kinship and Foster Care: Research report. Dunedin, New Zealand: Children's Issues Centre, University of Otago

C11

Spence N (2004) 'Kinship Care in Australia' *Child Abuse Review* 13 (4)

C12

Statistics New Zealand (2002) *New Zealand Official Year Book 2002*. Wellington: Bateman Publishers

C13

Stelmaszuk ZW (1999) 'The Continuing Role of Kinship Care in a Changing Society' in Greeff R (ed), *Fostering Kinship: An international perspective on kinship foster care*. Aldershot: Ashgate

C14

Worral J (2001) 'Kinship Care of the Abused Child: The New Zealand experience' *Child Welfare* 80 (5)

D1

Berridge D (1997) *Foster Care: A research review*. London: HMSO

D2

Broad B (ed) (2001) *Kinship Care: The placement choice for children and young people*. Lyme Regis: Russell House Publishing

D3

Broad B (2004) 'Kinship Care for Children in the UK: Messages from research, lessons for policy and practice' *European Journal of Social Work* 7 (2)

D4

Chand A (2000) 'The Over-representation of Black Children in the Child Protection System: Possible causes, consequences and solutions' *Child & Family Social Work* 5 (1)

D5

Clarke L and Cains H (2001) 'Grandparents and the Care of Children: the Research Evidence' in Broad B (ed), *Kinship Care: The placement choice for children and young people*. Russell House Publishing

D6

Department of Health (1991) *Patterns and Outcomes on Child Placement*. London: Department of Health, HMSO

D7

Department of Health (1995) *Child Protection: Messages from research*. London: Department of Health, HMSO

D8

Department of Health and Social Security (1985) *Social Work Decisions in Child Care: Recent research findings and their implications*. London: DHSS, HMSO

D9

Flynn R (2000) *Kinship Foster Care.* (Highlight 179). London: National Children's Bureau

D10

Flynn R (2002) 'Research Review: Kinship foster care' *Child & Family Social Work* 7 (4)

D11

Gulbenkian Foundation (1995) *Children and Violence: Report of the commission on children and violence*. London: Gulbenkian Foundation

D12

Holman R (1973) *Trading in Children*. London: Routledge and Kegan Paul

D13

Hunt J, Waterhouse S and Lutman E (forthcoming) *Keeping them in the Family: Outcomes for abused and neglected children placed with family or friends carers through care proceedings*. London: Jessica Kingsley

D14

Quinton D, Rushton A, Dance C and Mayes D (1997) 'Contact Between Children Placed Away from Home and their Birth Parents: Research issues and evidence' *Clinical Child Psychology and Psychiatry* 2 (3)

D15

Richards A and Tapsfield R (2003) *Funding Family and Friends Care: The way forward*. London: Family Rights Group

D16

Sinclair I (2005) *Fostering Now: Messages from research*. London: Jessica Kingsley

D17

Thoburn J (1996) 'The Research Evidence of the Importance of Links with Relatives when Children Are in Care' in, The Grandparents Federation (ed), *The Children Act 1989: What's in it for Grandparents?* Harlow: The Grandparents Federation

D18

Triseliotis J (1989) 'Foster Care Outcomes: A review of key research findings' *Adoption and Fostering* 13 (3)

D19

Utting D (1995) *Family and Parenthood: Supporting families, preventing breakdown*. York: Joseph Rowntree Foundation

D20
Waterhouse S (2001) 'Keeping Children in Kinship Placements within Court Proceedings' in Broad B (ed), *Kinship Care: The Placement choice for children and young people*. Russell House Publishing

D21
Waterhouse S and Brocklesby E (1999) 'Placement Choices for Children: Giving more priority to kinship placements?' in Greeff R (ed), *Fostering Kinship: An international perspective on kinship foster care*. Aldershot: Ashgate

D22
Wheal A (2001): 'Family and Friends Who Are Carers: A framework for success' in Broad B (ed), *Kinship Care: The placement choice for children and young people*. Lyme Regis: Russell House Publishing

D23
Wilson K, Sinclair I, Taylor C, Pithouse A and Sellick C (2004) *Fostering Success: An exploration of the research literature in foster care*. (Knowledge Review 5.) London: Social Care Institute for Excellence

E1
Barn R (1993) *Black Children in the Public Care System*. London: Batsford

E2
Barn R, Sinclair R and Ferdinand D (1997) *Acting on Principle: An examination of race and ethnicity in social services provision for children and families*. London: BAAF

E3
Bebbington A and Miles J (1989) 'The Background of Children Who Enter Local Authority Care' *British Journal of Social Work* 19 (5)

E4
Bell M (1999) *Child Protection: Families and the conference process*. Aldershot: Ashgate

E5
Biehal N, Clayden J, Stein M and Wade J (1995) *Moving On: Young people and leaving care schemes*. London: HMSO

E6
Bignall T and Butt J (2002) *Get Something Positive Done: Supporting black and minority ethnic families through family group conferencing: the experience of Lambeth Social Services Department*. London: REU

E7
Bullock R, Gooch D and Little M (1998) *Children Going Home: The reunification of families*. Aldershot: Ashgate

E8
Bullock R, Little M and Millham S (1993) Going Home: The return of children separated from their families. Aldershot: Dartmouth

E9
Burghes L, Clarke L and Cronin N (1997) *Fathers and Fatherhood in Britain*. London: Family Policy Studies Centre

E10
Cleaver H (2000) *Fostering Family Contact: A study of children, parents and foster carers*. London: The Stationery Office

E11
Cleaver H and Freeman P (1995) *Parental Perspectives in Cases of Suspected Child Abuse.* London: HMSO

E12
Crow G and Marsh P (1997) *Family Group Conferences, Partnership and Child Welfare: A research report on four pilot projects in England and Wales.* Sheffield: University of Sheffield

E13
Department for Education and Skills (2006b) *Referrals, Assessments and Children and Young People on Child Protection Registers, England – Year ending 31 March 2006.* (SFR 45/2006). London: DfES. Online version available at www.dfes.gov.uk/rsgateway/DB/SFR/s000692/index.shtml

E14
Dorling D, Rigby J, Wheeler B, Ballas D, Thomas B, Famy E, Gordon D and Lupton R (2007) *Poverty, Wealth and Place in Britain 1968 to 2005.* Bristol: The Policy Press for the Joseph Rowntree Foundation

E15
Farmer E (2001) 'Children Reunited with their Parents: A review of research findings' in Broad B (ed), *Kinship Care: The placement choice for children and young people.* Lyme Regis: Russell House Publishing

E16
Farmer E and Owen M (1995) *Child Protection: Private risks and public remedies.* London: HMSO

E17
Fisher M, Marsh P, Phillips D and Sainsbury E (1986) *In and Out of Care: The experiences of children, parents and social workers.* London: Batsford

E18
Freeman P and Hunt J (1999) *Parental Perspectives on Care Proceedings.* London: The Stationery Office

E19
Gregg P, Harkness S and Machin S (1999) *Child Development and Family Income.* York: Joseph Rowntree Foundation

E20
Hunt J (2003) *Family and Friends Care: Scoping paper for the Department of Health.* London: Department of Health. Online version available at www.dfes.gov.uk/childrenandfamilies/cfcirculars.shtml

E21
Hunt J and Macleod A (1999) *The Best-laid Plans: Outcomes of judicial decisions in child protection proceedings.* London: HMSO

E22
Hunt J, Macleod A and Thomas C (1999) *The Last Resort: Child protection, the courts and the 1989 Children Act.* London: The Stationery Office

E23
Laming H (2003) *The Victoria Climbié Inquiry: Report of an inquiry by Lord Laming.* London: HMSO

E24
Lupton C (1985) *Moving Out: Older teenagers leaving residential care.* Portsmouth: Social Services Research and Information Unit, University of Portsmouth

E25
Lupton C, Barnard S and Swall-Yarrington M (1995) *Family Planning? An evaluation of the family group conference model.* Portsmouth: Social Services Research and Information Unit, University of Portsmouth

E26
Lupton C and Stevens M (1997) *Family Outcomes: Following through on family group conferences.* Portsmouth: Social Services Research and Information Unit, University of Portsmouth

E27
Marsh P and Crow G (1998) *Family Group Conferences in Child Welfare.* Oxford: Blackwell Science

E28
Matheson J and Babb P (2000) *Social Trends 32.* London: Office for National Statistics, Stationery Office. Online version available at www.statistics.gov.uk

E29
Modood T, Berthoud R, Lakey J, Nazroo J, Smith P, Virdee S and Beishon S (1997) *Ethnic Minorities in Britain: Diversity and disadvantage – fourth national survey of ethnic minorities.* London: Policy Studies Institute

E30
Moore R (2000) 'Material Deprivation amongst Ethnic Minority and White Children: The evidence of the sample of anonymised records' in Bradshaw J and Sainsbury R (eds), *Experiencing Poverty.* Aldershot: Ashgate

E31
Morgan R (2006) *About Social Workers: A children's views report.* Newcastle: Office of the Children's Rights Director, Commission for Social Care Inspection

E32
Morrow V (1998) *Understanding Families: Children's perspectives.* London: National Children's Bureau

E33
National Statistics/Commission for Social Care Inspection (2006) *Social Services Performance Assessment Framework Indicators: Children 2005-2006.* London: CSCI

E34
National Statistics/Department for Education and Skills (2005) *Statistics of Education: Children looked after by local authorities, year ending 31 March 2004. Volume 1: Commentary and national tables.* Norwich: DfES, HMSO

E35
Oppenheim C and Harker L (1996) *Poverty: The facts.* London: Child Poverty Action Group

E36
Packman J, Randall J and Jacques N (1986) *Who Needs Care? Social work decisions about children.* Oxford: Basil Blackwell

E37
Phillips C (2006) *Kinship Care – Submission Children in Care Green Paper Team.* London: Office of the Children's Commissioner

E38
Platt L (2007) *Poverty and Ethnicity in the UK*. Bristol/York: The Policy Press/Joseph Rowntree Foundation

E39
Preston G (ed) (2005) *At Greatest Risk: The children most likely to be poor*. London: Child Poverty Action Group

E40
Prior D and Paris A (2005) *Preventing Children's Involvement in Crime and Antisocial Behaviour – A literature review*. (Paper produced for the DfES for the National Evaluation of the Children's Fund.) Birmingham: Institute of Applied Social Studies, Birmingham University

E41
Pulling J and Summerfield C (eds) (1997) *Social Focus on Families*. London: Office for National Statistics, The Stationery Office

E42
Richards A and Ince L (2000) *Overcoming the Obstacles, Looked After Children: Quality services for black and minority ethnic children and their families*. London: Family Rights Group

E43
Russell C (1995) *Parenting the Second Time Around: Grandparents as carers of young relatives in child protection cases*. (Unpublished dissertation.) University of East Anglia

E44
Ryburn M (1995) 'Adopted Children's Identity and Information Needs' *Children and Society* 9 (3)

E45
Sinclair I, Gibbs I and Wilson K (2004) *Foster Placements: Why they succeed and why they fail*. London: Jessica Kingsley

E46
Sinclair I, Wilson K and Gibbs I (2000) *Supporting Foster Placements. Second report to the Department of Health*. York: Social Work Research and Development Unit, University of York

E47
Smith L and Hennessy J (1999) *Making a Difference: Essex family group conference project; research findings and practice issues*. Chelmsford: Essex County Council Social Services Department

E48
Thoburn J, Lewis A and Shemmings D (1995) *Paternalism or Partnership? Family involvement in the child protection process*. London: HMSO

E49
Trasler G (1960) *In Place of Parents*. London: Routledge and Kegan Paul

E50
Trent J (1989) *Homeward Bound: The rehabilitation of children to their birth parents*. Ilford: Barnardo's

E51
Triseliotis J (1980) *New Developments in Foster Care and Adoption*. London: Routledge and Kegan Paul

E52
Walton E, Fraser M, Lewis R, Pecora P and Walton W (1993) 'In-home Family-focussed Reunification: An experimental study' *Child Welfare* 72 (5)

E53
Wedge P and Mantle G (1991) *Sibling Groups and Social Work: A study of children referred for permanent family placement.* Aldershot: Avebury

F1
Altshuler SJ (1998) 'Child Well-being in Kinship Foster Care: Similar to, or different from, non-related foster care?' *Children and Youth Services Review* 20 (5)

F2
Altshuler SJ (1999) 'The Well-being of Children in Kinship Foster Care' in Gleeson JP and Hairston CF (eds), *Kinship Care: Improving practice through research.* Washington DC: Child Welfare League of America

F3
Barth RP, Courtney ME, Berrick JD and Albert V (1994) *From Child Abuse to Permanency Planning: Child welfare services, pathways and placements.* New York: Aldine de Gruyter

F4
Berrick JD (2000) 'What Works in Kinship Care' in Kluger MP, Alexander G and Curtis PA (eds), *What Works in Child Welfare.* Washington DC: Child Welfare League of America Press

F5
Berrick JD, Barth R and Needell B (1994) 'A Comparison of Kinship Foster Homes and Foster Family Homes: Implications for kinship homes as family preservation' *Children and Youth Services Review* 16 (1-2)

F6
Connolly M (2003) *Kinship Care – A selected literature review.* New Zealand: Department of Child, Youth and Family. Online version available at www.cyf.govt.nz/documents/KinshipCare.pdf

F7
Courtney ME (1994) 'Factors Associated with the Reunification of Foster Children with their Families' *Social Service Review* 68 (1)

F8
Courtney ME and Needell B (1997) 'Outcomes of Kinship Care: Lessons from California' in Barth RP, Berrick JD and Gilbert N (eds), *Child Welfare Research Review: Volume 2.* New York: Columbia University Press

F9
Crampton D (2001) 'Making Sense of Foster Care: An evaluation of family group decision making in Kent County, Michigan' *Dissertation Abstracts International* 62 (10), UMI Publication number AAT 3029324

F10
Crumbley J and Little RL (1997) *Relatives Raising Children: An overview of kinship care.* Washington DC: Child Welfare League of America

F11
Doolan M and Nixon P (2003) 'The Importance of Kinship Care' *Social Work Now* 25 (September)

F12
Dubowitz H, Feigelman S and Zuravin S (1993) 'A Profile of Kinship Care' *Child Welfare* 72 (3)

F13
Ernst JS (1999) 'Whanau Knows Best: Kinship care in New Zealand' in Hegar R and Scannapieco M (eds), *Kinship Foster Care: Policy, practice and research*. New York: Oxford University Press

F14
General Accounting Office (1999) *Foster Care: Kinship care quality and permanency issues*. (Report to the Chairman, Subcommittee of Human Resources, Committee on Ways and Means, US House of Representatives.) Washington DC: General Accounting Office

F15
George S and van Oudenhoven N (2002) *Stakeholders in Foster Care: An international comparative study*. Louvain (Belgium) and Apeldoorn (Netherlands): IFCO and Garant Publisher

F16
Gleeson JP (1999b) 'Kinship Care as a Child Welfare Service: What do we really know?' in Gleeson JP and Hairston CF (eds), *Kinship Care: Improving practice through research*. Washington DC: Child Welfare League of America

F17
Gleeson JP and Hairston CF (1999) 'Future Directions for Research on Kinship Care' in Gleeson JP and Hairston CF (eds), *Kinship Care: Improving practice through research*. Washington DC: Child Welfare League of America

F18
Gunderson K, Cahn K and Wirth J (2003) 'The Washington State Long-term Outcome Study' *Protecting Children* 18 (1-2)

F19
Hassall IB and Maxwell GM (1991) 'The Family Group Conference' in Maxwell GM (ed) *An Appraisal of the First Year of the Children, Young Persons and their Families Act 1989*. Wellington, New Zealand: Office of the Commissioner for Children

F20
Hegar R (1999) 'The Cultural Roots of Kinship Care' in Hegar R and Scannapieco M (eds), *Kinship Foster Care: Policy, practice and research*. New York: Oxford University Press

F21
Hegar R and Scannapieco M (1995) 'From Family Duty to Family Policy: The evolution of kinship care' *Child Welfare* 74 (1)

F22
Holland S, Faulkner A and Perez-del-Aguila R (2005) 'Promoting Stability and Continuity of Care for Looked After Children: A survey and critical review' *Child & Family Social Work* 10 (1)

F23
Iglehart A (1994) 'Kinship Foster Care: Placement, service and outcome issues' *Children and Youth Services Review* 16 (1-2)

F24
Iglehart AP (1995) 'Readiness for Independence: Comparison of foster care, kinship care and non-foster care adolescents' *Children and Youth Services Review* 17 (3)

F25
Jendrek MP (1994) 'Grandparents Who Parent their Grandchildren: Circumstances and decisions' *The Gerontologist* 34 (2)

F26
Johnson EI and Walfogel J (2002) 'Parental Incarceration: Recent trends and implications for child welfare' *Social Service Review* 76 (3)

F27
Johnson H (1995) *Traditions in a New Time: Stories of grandmothers.* (PhD Thesis.) New York: Colombia University

F28
Landsverk J, Davis I, Ganger W, Newton R and Johnson I (1996) 'Impact of Child Psychosocial Functioning on Reunification from Out-of-Home Placement' *Children and Youth Services Review* 18 (4-5)

F29
Lee CD and Ayon C (2004) 'Is the Client-Worker Relationship Associated with Better Outcomes in Mandated Child Abuse Cases?' *Research on Social Work Practice* 14 (5)

F30
Leos-Urbel J, Bess R and Geen R (2000) *State Policies for Assessing and Supporting Kinship Foster Parents.* Washington DC: The Urban Institute. Online version available at www.urban.org/url.cfm?ID=409609

F31
Le Prohn NS (1994) 'The Role of the Kinship Foster Parent: A comparison of the role conceptions of relative and non-relative foster parents' *Children and Youth Services Review* 16 (1-2)

F32
Lewis RE and Fraser M (1987) 'Blending Informal and Formal Helping Networks in Foster Care' *Children and Youth Services Review* 9 (3)

F33
Lorkovich TW, Piccola T, Groza V, Brindo ME and Marks J (2004) 'Kinship Care and Permanence: Guiding principles for policy and practice' *Families in Society* 85 (2)

F34
McFadden E (1998) 'Kinship Care in the United States' *Adoption and Fostering* 22 (3)

F35
McFadden E and Downs S (1995) 'Family Continuity: The new paradigm in permanence planning' *Community Alternatives* 7 (1)

F36
Malos E and Bullard E (1991) *Custodianship: The care of other people's children.* London: HMSO

F37
Maxwell GM and Morris A (1992) 'The Family Group Conference: A new paradigm for making decisions about children and young people' *Children Australia* 17 (4)

F38
Needell B, Webster D and Barth RP (1996) *Performance Indicators for Child Welfare Services in California: 1995.* (Unpublished report.) Berkeley: Child Welfare Research Centre, University of California

F39
Pecora PJ, Le Prohn NS and Nasuti JJ (1999) 'Role Perceptions of Kinship and Other Foster Parents in Family Foster Care' in Hegar R and Scannapieco M (eds), *Kinship Foster Care: Policy, practice and research.* New York: Oxford University Press

F40
Rodning C, Beckwith L, and Howard J (1991) 'Quality of Attachment and Home Environments in Children Prenatally Exposed to PCP and Cocaine' *Development and Psychopathology* 3 (4)

F41
Scannapieco M (1999) 'Kinship Care in the Public Child Welfare System: A systematic review of the research' in Hegar R and Scannapieco M (eds), *Kinship Foster Care: Policy, practice and research.* New York: Oxford University Press

F42
Scannapieco M and Hegar RL (1999) 'Kinship Foster Care In Context' in Hegar R and Scannapieco M (eds), *Kinship Foster Care: Policy, practice and research.* New York: Oxford University Press

F43
Schofield V (2005) 'Third Generation Parenting' *Social Work Now* 30 (April)

F44
Schwartz AE (2002) 'Societal Value and the Funding of Kinship Care' *Social Service Review* 76 (3)

F45
Sheindlin JB (1994) 'Paying Grandparents to Keep Kids in Limbo' (op-ed page, *The New York Times,* 29 August) cited in McLean B and Thomas TC (1996) 'Informal and Formal Kinship Care Populations: A study in contrasts' *Child Welfare* 75 (5)

F46
Starr RH, Dubowitz H, Harrington D and Feigelman S (1999) 'Behaviour Problems of Teens in Kinship Care' in Hegar R and Scannapieco M (eds), *Kinship Foster Care: Policy, practice and research.* New York: Oxford University Press

F47
Strozier A, Elrod B, Beiler P, Smith A and Carter K (2004) 'Developing a Network of Support for Relative Caregivers' *Children and Youth Services Review* 26 (7)

F48
Szolnoki J and Cahn K (2002) *African American Kinship Caregivers: Principles for developing supportive programs.* Seattle, WA: University of Washington School of Social Work, Northwest Institute for Children and Families

F49
Testa MF (1997) 'Kinship Foster Care in Illinois' in Barth RP, Berrick JD and Gilbert N (eds), *Child Welfare Research Review: Volume 2*. New York: Columbia University Press

F50
Testa MF and Shook Slack K (2002) 'The Gift of Kinship Foster Care' *Children and Youth Services Review* 24 (1-2)

F51
Testa MF, Shook K, Cohen L and Woods M (1996) 'Permanency Planning Options for Children in Formal Kinship Care' *Child Welfare* 75 (6)

F52
Thornton C (1993) *Family Group Conferences: A literature review*. Lower Hutt, New Zealand: Practitioners' Publishing

F53
Thornton J (1987) *An Investigation into the Nature of the Kinship Foster Home.* (PhD dissertation.) New York: Wurzweiler School of Social Work, Yeshiva University

F54
Thornton JL (1991) 'Permanency Planning for Children in Kinship Foster Homes' *Child Welfare* 70 (5)

F55
Titcomb A and LeCroy C (2003) 'Evaluation of Arizona's Family Group Decision Making Program' *Protecting Children* 18 (1-2)

F56
Weinstein EA (1960) *The Self-image of the Foster Child*. New York: Russell Sage Foundation

F57
Woodworth R (1996) 'You're Not Alone ... You're One in a Million' *Child Welfare* 75 (6)

F58
Wulczyn F and George R (1992) 'Foster Care in New York and Illinois: The challenge of rapid change' *Social Service Review* 66 (2)

F59
Yorker BC, Kelley SJ, Whitley D, Lewis A, Magis J, Bergeron A and Napier C (1998) 'Custodial Relationships of Grandparents Raising Grandchildren: Results of a home-based intervention study' *Juvenile and Family Court Journal* 49 (2)

F60
Zimmerman E, Daykin D, Moore V, Wuu C and Li J (1998) *Kinship and Non-kinship Foster Care in New York City: Pathways and outcomes*. New York: United Way of New York City

F61
Zuravin S, Benedict M and Somerfield M (1997) 'Child Maltreatment in Family Foster Care: Foster home correlates' in Barth RP, Berrick JD and Gilbert N (eds), *Child Welfare Research Review: Volume 2*. New York: Columbia University Press

G1

Adams R (2003) *Social Work and Empowerment*. Basingstoke: Palgrave Macmillan

G2

Braye S and Preston-Shoot M (1995) *Empowering Practice in Social Care*. Buckingham: Open University Press

G3

Gleeson JP (1996) 'Kinship Care as a Child Welfare Service: The policy debate in an era of welfare reform' *Child Welfare* 75 (5)

G4

Greeff R (1999) 'Kinship, Fostering, Obligations and the State' in Greeff R (ed) *Fostering Kinship: An international perspective on kinship foster care*. Aldershot: Ashgate

G5

Hill M and Aldgate J (1996) *Child Welfare Services: Developments in law, policy, practice and research*. London: Jessica Kingsley

G6

Lawler J (2000) 'The Rise of Managerialism in Social Work' in Harlow E and Lawler J (eds), *Management, Social Work and Change*. Ashgate: Aldershot

G7

Littlechild B (2004) 'Social Work in the UK: The professional debate in relation to values and managerialism' *Inter-University Centre (IUC) Journal of Social Work Theory and Practice* 7 (Spring)

G8

Lupton C and Nixon P (1999) *Empowering Practice? A critical appraisal of the family group conference approach*. Bristol: The Policy Press

G9

National Foster Care Association (2000) *Family and Friends: Carers' handbook and Family and Friends: Social workers' training guide*. London: NFCA

G10

Nixon P (2001) 'Making Kinship Partnerships Work: Examining family group conferences' in Broad B (ed), *Kinship Care: The placement of choice for children and young people*. Lyme Regis: Russell House Publishing

G11

Nixon P (2007) 'Seen but Not Heard? Children and Young People's Participation in Family Group Decision Making: Concepts and practice issues' *Protecting Children* 22 (1)

G12

O'Brien V (2000) 'Relative Care: A different type of foster care – implications for practice' in Kelly G and Gilligan R (eds), *Issues in Foster Care: Policy, practice and research*. London: Jessica Kingsley

G13

Parton N (2001) 'Risk and Professional Judgement' in Cull L and Roche J (eds), *The Law and Social Work: Contemporary issues for practice*. Basingstoke: Open University, Palgrave

G14
Smale G, Tuson G and Statham D (2000) *Social Work and Social Problems: Working towards social inclusion and social change.* Basingstoke: Palgrave Macmillan

G15
Testa MF and Rolock N (1999) 'Professional Foster Care: A future worth pursuing?' *Child Welfare* 78 (1)

G16
Wheal A and Waldman J (1997) *Friends and Family as Carers: Identifying the training needs of carers and social workers.* London: National Foster Care Association

H1
Children Act 1989. London: HMSO

H2
Children Act 2004. London: HMSO

H3
Children (Private Arrangements for Fostering) Regulations 2005, SI No.1533. London: HMSO

H4
Community Care (2005) 'Court action will test discriminatory fostering payments to kinship carers' (26 August)

H5
Department for Education and Skills (2003) *Every Child Matters.* London: The Stationery Office (Cm 5860)

H6
Department for Education and Skills (2006) *Children Looked After in England (Including Adoption and Care Leavers), 2005-2006.* (SFR44/2006). London: DfES. Online version available at www.dfes.gov.uk/rsgateway/DB/SFR/s000691/index.shtml

H7
Department for Education and Skills (2007) *Care Matters: Time for Change.* London: The Stationery Office (Cm 7137)

H8
Department of Health (1989) *The Care of Children: Principles and practice in regulations and guidance.* London: Department of Health, HMSO

H9
Department of Health and Department for Education and Skills (2006) *Options for Excellence: Building the social care workforce of the future.* London: Department of Health

references - alphabetical

Adams R (2003) Social Work and Empowerment. Basingstoke: Palgrave and Macmillan G

Aldgate J and McIntosh M (2006) Looking After the Family: A study of children looked after in kinship care in Scotland. Edinburgh: Social Work Inspection Agency A

Altshuler SJ (1998) 'Child Well-being in Kinship Foster Care: Similar to, or different from, non-related foster care' Children and Youth Services Review 20 (5) F

Altshuler SJ (1999) 'The Well-being of Children in Kinship Foster Care' in Gleeson JP and Hairston CF (eds), Kinship Care: Improving practice through Research. Washington, DC: Child Welfare League of America F

Altshuler SJ and Gleeson JP (1999) 'Completing the Evaluation Triangle for the Next Century: Measuring child "well-being" in family foster care' Child Welfare 78 (1) B

Barn R (1993) Black Children in the Public Care System. London: Batsford E

Barn R, Sinclair R and Ferdinand D (1997) Acting on Principle: An examination of race and ethnicity in social services provision for children and families. London: BAAF E

Barth RP, Courtney ME, Berrick JD and Albert V (1994) From Child Abuse to Permanency Planning: Child welfare services, pathways and placements. New York: Aldine de Gruyter F

Bebbington A and Miles J (1989) 'The Background of Children Who Enter Local Authority Care' British Journal of Social Work 19 (9) E

Beeman S and Boisen L (1999) 'Child Welfare Professionals' Attitudes Towards Kinship Foster Care' Child Welfare 78 (3) B

Beeman S, Wattenberg E, Boisen L and Bullerdick S (1996) Kinship Foster Care in Minnesota. Minnesota: Center for Advanced Studies in Child Welfare, University of Minnesota School of Social Work B

Bell M (1999) Child Protection: Families and the conference process – evaluative research in social work. Aldershot: Ashgate E

Benedict M and White R (1991) 'Factors Associated with Foster Care Length of Stay' Child Welfare 50 (1) B

Benedict M, Zuravin S and Stallings R (1996) 'Adult Functioning of Children Who Lived in Kin Versus Non-relative Family Foster Homes' Child Welfare 75 (5) B

Bergerhed E (1995) 'Kinship and Network Care in Sweden' in Thelen H (ed) Foster Children in a Changing World: Documentation of the 1994 European IFCO conference in Berlin. Berlin: Arbeitskreis Zur Forderung Von Pflegekindern E.V. C

Berrick JD (1997) 'Assessing the Quality of Care in Kinship and Foster Family Care' Family Relations 46 (3) B

Berrick JD (1998) 'When Children Cannot Remain Home: Foster family care and kinship care' Protecting Children from Abuse and Neglect 8 (1)

Berrick JD (2000) 'What Works in Kinship Care' in Kluger MP, Alexander G and Curtis PA (eds), What Works in Child Welfare. Washington DC: Child Welfare League of America Press F

Berrick JD, Barth R and Needell B (1994) 'A Comparison of Kinship Foster Homes and Foster Family Homes: Implications for kinship homes as family preservation' Child Welfare Research Review 16 F

Berrick JD and Needell B (1999) 'Recent Trends in Kinship Care: Public policy, payments and outcomes for children' in Curtis PA and Grady D (eds), *The Foster Care Crisis: Translating research into practice and policy.* Lincoln, NB: Child Welfare League of America and University of Nebraska Press B

Berrick JD, Needell B and Barth RP (1998) 'Kin as a Family and Child Welfare Resource: The child welfare workers perspective' in Hegar RL and Scannapieco M (eds), *Kinship Foster Care: Practice, policy and research.* New York: Oxford University Press B

Berridge D (1997) *Foster Care: A research review.* London: HMSO D

Berridge D and Cleaver H (1987) *Foster Home Breakdown.* Oxford: Blackwell A

Biehal N, Clayden J, Stein M and Wade J (1995) *Moving On: Young people and leaving care schemes.* London: HMSO E

Bignall T and Butt J (2002) *Get Something Positive Done: Supporting black and minority ethnic families through family group conferencing: the experience of Lambeth Social Services Department.* London: REU E

Billing A, Ehrle J and Kortenkamp K (2002) *Children Cared for by Relatives: What do we know about their well-being? New Federalism: National survey of America's families, Series B (B-46).* Washington DC: The Urban Institute B

Bonecutter FJ (1999) 'Defining Best Practice in Kinship Care Through Research and Demonstration' in Gleeson JP and Hairston CF (eds) *Kinship Care: Improving practice through research.* Washington DC: Child Welfare League of America B

Braye S and Preston-Shoot M (1995) *Empowering Practice in Social Care.* Buckingham: Open University Press G

Broad B (ed) (2001) *Kinship Care: The Placement Choice for Children and Young People.* Lyme Regis: Russell House Publishing D

Broad B, Hayes R and Rushforth C (2001) *Kith and Kin: Kinship care for vulnerable young people.* National Children's Bureau, Joseph Rowntree Foundation A

Brooks D (1999) 'Kinship Care and Substance-exposed Children' *The Source* (Bi-annual magazine of The National Abandoned Infants Assistance Resource Center) 9 (1) B

Brooks D and Barth R (1998) 'Characteristics and Outcomes of Drug-exposed and Non-drug Exposed Children in Kinship Care and Non-relative Foster Care' *Children and Youth Services Review,* 20 (6) B

Bullock R, Gooch D and Little M (1998) *Children Going Home: The reunification of families.* Aldershot: Dartmouth E

Bullock R, Little M and Millham S (1993) *Going Home: The return of children separated from their families.* Aldershot: Dartmouth E

Burghes L, Clarke L and Cronin N (1997) *Fathers and Fatherhood in Britain.* London: Family Policy Study Centre E

Burnette D (1999) 'Social relationships of Latino grandparent caregivers: A role theory perspective' *The Gerontologist* 39(1) B

Carpenter S and Clyman R (2004) 'The Long-term Emotional and Physical Well-being of Women Who Have Lived in Kinship Care' *Children and Youth Services Review* 26 (7) B

Chalfie D (1994) *Going It Alone: A closer look at grandparents parenting children.*

Washington DC: American Association of Retired Persons B

Chand A (2000) 'The Over-representation of Black Children in the Child Protection System: Possible causes, consequences and solutions' *Child and Family Social Work* 5 (1) D

Children Act (England and Wales) (1989) London: HMSO H

Children Act 2004 (England) London: HMSO H

Children (Private Arrangements for Fostering) Regulations 2005, SI No.1533. London: HMSO H

Chipungu S and Everett J (1998) *Children Placed in Foster Care with Relatives: A Multistate Study.* Washington DC: US Department of Health and Human Services B

Cimmarusti R, Derezotes DM, Skolec J and Dannenbring-Carlson D (2000) *Kinship Caregiver Burden.* Urbana-Champaign, IL: University of Illinois at Urbana-Champaign, School of Social Work, Children and Family Research Center B

Cleaver H (2000) *Fostering Family Contact: A study of children, parents and foster carers.* London: The Stationery Office E

Cleaver H and Freeman P (1995) *Parental Perspectives in Cases of Suspected Child Abuse.* London: HMSO E

Community Care (2005) 'Court action will test discriminatory fostering payments to kinship carers' (26 August) H

Connolly M (2003) *Kinship Care – A selected literature review.* New Zealand: Department of Child, Youth and Family. Online version available at: www.cyfs.govt.nz F

Cook R and Ciarico J (1998) (unpublished) *Analysis of Kinship Care Data from the US DHHA National Study of Protective, Preventive and Reunification Services Delivered to Children and Their Families.* B

Courtney M and Needell B (1997) 'Outcomes of Kinship Care: Lessons from California' in Barth RP, Berrick JD and Gilbert N (eds) *Child Welfare Research Review: Volume 2.* New York: Columbia University Press F

Courtney ME (1994) 'Factors Associated With the Reunification of Foster Children With Their Families' *Social Service Review* 68 F

Crampton D (2001) 'Making Sense of Foster Care: An evaluation of family group decision making in Kent County, Michigan' *Dissertation Abstracts International* 62 (10), UMI Publication number AAT 3029324 F

Crow G and Marsh P (1997) *Family Group Conferences, Partnership and Child Welfare: A research report on four pilot projects in England and Wales.* Sheffield: University of Sheffield E

Crumbley J and Little RL (1997) *Relatives Raising Children: An overview of kinship care.* Washington DC: Child Welfare League of America Press F

Department for Education and Skills (2003) *Every Child Matters.* London: The Stationery Office (Cm 5860) H

Department for Education and Skills (2006) *Options for Excellence.* London: DfES and Department of Health H

Department for Education and Skills (2006a) *Referrals, Assessments, and Children and Young People on Child Protection Registers, England – Year ending 31 March 2006.* Online version available at www.dfes.gov.uk/rsgateway/DB/SFR/s000692/index.shtml E

Department for Education and Skills (2007) *Care Matters: Time for Change.* London: The Stationery Office (Cm 7137) H

Department of Health (1989) *The Care of Children: Principles and practice in regulations and guidance.* London: Department of Health, HMSO H

Department of Health (1991) *Patterns and Outcomes on Child Placement.* London: Department of Health, HMSO D

Department of Health (1995) *Child Protection: Messages from research.* London: Department of Health, HMSO D

Department of Health and Social Security (1985) *Social Work Decisions in Child Care.* London: DHSS, HMSO D

Doolan M, Nixon P and Lawrence P (2004) *Growing Up in the Care of Relatives or Friends: Delivering best practice for children in family and friends care.* London: Family Rights Group A

Dorling D, Rigby J, Wheeler B, Ballas D, Thomas B, Famy E, Gordon D and Lupton R (2007) *Poverty, Wealth and Place in Britain 1968 to 2005.* JRF/Policy Press E

Dubowitz H (1990) *The Physical and Mental Health and Educational Status of Children Placed with Relatives: Final report.* Maryland, Baltimore MD: University of Maryland Medical School B

Dubowitz H, Feigelman S, Harrington D, Starr T, Zuravin S and Sawyer R (1994) 'Children in kinship care: How do they fare?' *Children and Youth Services Review* 16 B

Dubowitz H, Feigelman S and Zuravin S (1993) 'A Profile of Kinship Care' *Child Welfare* 72 F

Dubowitz H, Zuravin S, Starr R, Feigelman S and Harrington D (1993) `Behavioural Problems of Children in Kinship Care' *Journal of Behavioural and Developmental Paediatrics* 14 (6) B

Ehrle J, Green R and Clark R (2001) *Children Cared for by Relatives: Who are they and how are they faring.* Urban Institute. Online version available at http://newfederalism.urban.org B

Ehrle J and Kortenkamp K (2002) 'The Well-being of Children Involved With the Child Welfare System: A national overview' *New Federalism: National Survey of America's Families, Series B (B-43)* Washington DC: The Urban Institute B

Farmer E (2001) 'Children Reunified With Their Parents: A review of research findings' in Broad B (ed) *Kinship Care: The placement choice for children and young people.* Lyme Regis: Russell House Publishing E

Farmer E and Owen M (1995) *Child Protection: Private risks and public remedies.* London: HMSO E

Farmer R and Moyers S (2005) *Children Placed with Relatives and Friends: Placement Patterns and Outcomes.* (Report to the DfES) Bristol: School for Policy Studies, University of Bristol A

Fein E, Maluccio A, Hamilton J and Ward D (1983) 'After Foster Care: Outcomes of permanence planning for children' *Child Welfare* 6 B

Fisher M, Marsh P, Phillips D and Sainsbury E (1986) *In and Out of Care: The experiences of children, parents and social workers.* London: Batsford E

Fitzpatrick M and Reeve P (2003) 'Grandparents Raising Grandchildren: A new class of disadvantaged Australians' *Family Matters* 66 C

Flynn R (2000) *Kinship Foster Care. (Highlight 179)*. London: National
Children's Bureau D

Flynn R (2002) 'Research Review: Kinship foster care' *Child and Family Social
Work* 7 (4) D

Freeman P and Hunt J (1999) *Parental Perspectives on Care Proceedings*. London:
The Stationery Office E

Fuller-Thomson E (2000) 'African American Grandparents Raising
Grandchildren: A national profile of demographic and health characteristics'
Health & Social Work 25 B

Gabel G (1992) *Preliminary Report on Kinship Foster Family Profile*. New York:
Human Resources Administration, Child Welfare Administration B

Gaudin J and Sutphen R (1993) 'Foster Care vs Extended Family Care for
Children of Incarcerated Mothers' *Journal of Offender Rehabilitation* 19 (3/4) B

Gebel T (1996) 'Kinship Care and Non-relative Family Foster Care: A
comparison of caregiver attributes and attitude' *Child Welfare* 75 (5) B

General Accounting Office (1999) *Foster Care: Kinship care quality and
permanency issues (Report to the Chairman, Subcommittee of Human Resources,
Committee on Ways and Means, US House of Representatives)* Washington, DC:
General Accounting Office F

Gennaro S, York R and Dunphy P (1998) 'Vulnerable Infants: Kinship care
and health' *Pediatric Nursing* 24 (2) B

George S and van Oudenhoven N (2002) *Stakeholders in Foster Care: An
international comparative study*. Louvain (Belgium) and Apeldoorn
(Netherlands): IFCO and Garant Publishers F

Gibson PA (2002a) 'Caregiving Role Affects Family Relationships of African
American Grandmothers as New Mothers Again: A phenomenological
perspective' *Journal of Marital and Family Therapy* 28 B

Gibson PA (2002b) 'African American Grandmothers as Caregivers:
Answering the call to help their grandchildren' *Families and Society* 83 (1) B

Gleeson JP (1996) 'Kinship Care in Child Welfare Service: The policy debate
in an era of reform' *Child Welfare* 75 G

Gleeson JP (1999a) `Who Decides? Predicting caseworkers adoption and
guardianship discussions with kinship caregivers' in Gleeson JP and
Hairston CF (eds) *Kinship Care Improving Practice Through Research*. Washington
DC: Child Welfare League of America B

Gleeson JP (1999b) 'Kinship Care as a Child Welfare Service: What do we
really know?' in Gleeson JP and Hairston CF (eds) *Kinship Care Improving
Practice Through Research*. Washington DC: Child Welfare League of America F

Gleeson JP and Hairston CF (1999) 'Future Directions for Research on
Kinship Care' in Gleeson JP and Hairston CF (eds) *Kinship Care Improving
Practice Through Research*. Washington DC: Child Welfare League of America F

Goodman C, Potts M, Pasztor E and Scorzo D (2004) 'Grandmothers As
Kinship Caregivers: Private arrangements compared to public child welfare
oversight' *Children and Youth Services Review* 26 B

Grandparents Federation (1996) *Residence Order Allowance Survey*. Harlow:
Grandparents Federation A

Greeff R (1999) 'Kinship, Fostering, Obligations and the State' in Greef R (ed) *Fostering Kinship: An international perspective on kinship foster care*. Aldershot: Ashgate G

Gregg P, Harkness S and Machin S (1999) *Child Development and Family Income*. York: Joseph Rowntree Foundation E

Gulbenkien Foundation (1995) *Children and Violence: Report of the commission on children and violence*. London: Gulbenkien Foundation D

Gunderson K, Cahn K and Wirth J (2003) 'The Washington State Long-term Outcome Study' *Protecting Children* 18 (1&2) F

Hannah L and Pitman S (2000) *Oz Child's Kith and Kin Program*. Melbourne: Oz Child C

Harden AW, Clark RL and Maguire K (1997): *Informal and Formal Kinship Care*. Washington DC: US Department of Health and Human Services B

Harden B, Clyman R, Kriebel D and Lyons M (2004) 'Kith and Kin Care: Parental attitudes and resources of foster and relative caregivers' *Children and Youth Services Review* 26 (7) B

Harwin J, Owen M, Locke R and Forrester D (2001) *Making Care Orders Work: A study of care plans and their Implementation*. London: The Stationery Office A

Hassall IB and Maxwell GM (1991) 'The Family Group Conference' in Maxwell GM (ed) *An Appraisal of the First Year of the Children and Young Persons and their Families Act 1989*. Wellington, New Zealand: Officer for the Commissioner for Children F

Hatmaker C (1999) *Project REFRESH: Research and Evaluation of Foster Children's Reception into Environmentally Supportive Homes, Final Qualitative Report*. Oregon: Family Policy Program, Oregon State University B

Hegar RL (1993) 'Assessing Attachment, Permanence and Kinship in Choosing Permanent Homes' *Child Welfare* 72 B

Hegar R (1999) 'The Cultural Roots of Kinship Care' in Hegar R and Scannapieco M (eds) *Kinship Foster Care: Policy, practice and research*. New York: Oxford University Press F

Hegar R and Scannapieco M (1995) 'From Family Duty to Family Foster Care: The evolution of kinship care' *Child Welfare* 64 F

Helfinger C and Taylor-Richardson K (2004) 'Caregiver Strain in Families of Children With Serious Emotional Disturbance: Does relationship to child make a difference?' *Journal of Family Social Work* 8 (1) B

Henry, J (1999) 'Permanency Outcomes in Legal Guardianships of Abused and Neglected Children' *Families in Society* 80 (6) B

Hill M and Aldgate J (1996) *Child Welfare Services: Developments in law, policy, practice and research*. London: Jessica Kingsley Publishers G

Holland S, Faulkner A and Perez-del-Aguila R (2005) 'Promoting Stability and Continuity of Care for Looked After Children: A survey and critical review' *Child and Family Social Work* 10 (1) F

Holman R (1973) *Trading in Children*. London: Routledge and Kegan Paul D

Hunt J (2001) 'Kinship Care, Child Protection and the Courts' in Broad B (ed) *Kinship Care: The placement choice for children and young people*. Lyme Regis: Russell House Publishing A

Hunt J (2003) *Family and Friends Care: Scoping paper for the Department of Health*. London: Department of Health. Online version available at www.dfes.gov.uk/childrenandfamilies/cfcirculars.shtml

Hunt J and Macleod A (1999) *The Best-laid Plans: Outcomes of judicial decisions in child protection proceedings*. London: HMSO E

Hunt J, Macleod A and Thomas C (1999) *The Last Resort: Child protection, the courts and the 1989 Children Act*. London: The Stationery Office E

Hunt J, Waterhouse S and Lutman E (forthcoming) *Keeping Them in the Family: Outcomes for abused and neglected children placed with family or friends carers through care proceedings*. London: Jessica Kingsley

Iglehart A (1994) 'Kinship Foster Care: Placement, service and outcome issues' *Children and Youth Services Review* 16 (1-2) F

Iglehart AP (1995) 'Readiness for Independence: Comparison of foster care, kinship care and non-foster care adolescents' *Children and Youth Services Review* 17 (3) F

James S (2004) 'Why Do Foster Care Placements Disrupt? An investigation of the reasons for placement change in foster care' *Social Service Review* 78 (4) B

Jendrek MP (1994) 'Grandparents Who Parent Their Grandchildren: Circumstances and decisions' *The Gerontologist* 34 F

Johnson EI and Walfogel J (2002) 'Parental Incarceration: Recent trends and implications for child welfare' *Social Service Review* 76 F

Johnson H (1995) *Traditions in a New Time: Stories of grandmothers*. (PhD Thesis) New York: Colombia University

Kosenen M (1996) 'Maintaining sibling relationships-Neglected dimension in Child Care practice' *British Journal of Social Work* 26 A

Kosenen M (1999) 'Core and Kin Siblings: Foster children's changing families' in Mullender A (ed) *We Are Family: Sibling relationships in placement and beyond*. Nottingham: BAAF A

Landry-Meyer L and Newman B (2004) 'An Exploration of the Grandparent Caregiver Role' *Journal of Family Issues* 25 (8) B

Landsverk J, Newton R, Ganger W and Davis I (1996) 'Impact of Child Psychosocial Functioning on Reunification from Out of Home Placement' *Children and Youth Services Review* 18 (4/5) F

Laming H (2003) *The Victoria Climbié Inquiry: Report of an inquiry by Lord Laming*. London: HMSO E

Lawler J (2000) 'The Rise of Managerialism in Social Work' in Harlow E and Lawler L (eds) *Management, Social Work and Change*. Ashgate: Aldershot G

Laws S (2001) 'Looking After Children Within the Extended Family: Carers' views' in Broad B (ed) *Kinship Care: The placement choice for children and young people*. Dorset UK: Russell House Publishing Ltd. A

Laws S and Broad B (2000) *Looking After Children Within the Extended Family: Carers' views*. Leicester: Centre for Social Action, De Montford University A

Lee CD and Ayon C (2004) 'Is the Client-Worker Relationship Associated With Better Outcomes in Mandated Child Abuse Cases?' *Research in Social Work Practice* 14 (5) F

Leos-Urbel J, Bess R and Geen R (2000) *State Policies for Assessing and Supporting Kinship Foster Parents*. Washington DC: The Urban Institute Online version available at www.urban.org/url.cfmID=409609 F

Le Prohn NS (1993) *Relative Foster Parents: Role perceptions, motivation and agency satisfaction*. PhD dissertation, University of Washington, Seattle, Washington (cited in General Accounting Office (1999) *Foster Care: Kinship care quality and permanency Issues*.) B

Le Prohn NS (1994) 'The Role of the Kinship Foster Parent: A comparison of the role conceptions of relative and non-relative foster parents' *Social Services Review* 16 F

Le Prohn NS and Pecora P (1994) *Summary of the Casey Foster Parent Study.* Seattle, WA: Casey Family Program B

Lewis RE and Fraser M (1987) 'Blending Informal and Formal Helping Networks in Foster Care' *Children and Youth Service Review* 9 F

Link M (1996) 'Permanency Outcomes in Kinship Care: A study of children placed in kinship care in Erie County, New York' *Child Welfare* 75 B

Littlechild B (2004) 'Social Work in the UK: The professional debate in relation to values and manageralism' *Inter-University Centre (IUC) Journal of Social Work Theory and Practice* (7) G

Lorkovich T, Piccola T, Groza V, Brindo M and Marks J (2004) 'Kinship Care and Permanence: Guiding principles for policy and practice' *Families in Society: Journal for Contemporary Social Services* 82 (2) F

Lupton C (1985) *Moving Out: The experiences of older teenagers leaving care.* Portsmouth: Social Services Research and Information Unit (SSRIU), University of Portsmouth E

Lupton C, Barnard S, and Swall-Yarrington M (1995) *Family Planning? An evaluation of the FGC model.* Portsmouth: University of Portsmouth (SSRIU Report No. 31) E

Lupton C and Nixon P (1999) *Empowering Practice? A critical appraisal of the family group conference approach.* Bristol: Policy Press G

Lupton C and Stevens M (1997) *Family Outcomes: Following through on family group conferences.* Portsmouth: University of Portsmouth (SSRIU Report No. 34) E

McFadden E (1998) 'Kinship Care in the United States' *Adoption and Fostering* 22 (3) F

McFadden E and Downs S (1995) 'Family Continuity: The new paradigm in permanency planning' *Community Alternatives* 7 (1) F

McGlone F, Park A and Smith K (1998) *Families and Kinship: Family and parenthood policy and practice.* London: Family Policy Studies Centre A

McLean B and Thomas R (1996) 'Informal and Formal Kinship Care Populations: A study in contrasts' *Child Welfare*, 75 (5) A

Main R, Ehrle Macomber J and Green R (2006) *Trends in Service Receipt: Children in kinship care gaining ground. New Federalism: National survey of America's families, Series B* (B-68). Washington DC: The Urban Institute B

Malos E and Bullard E (1991) *Custodianship: The care of other people's children.* London: HMSO F

Marsh P and Crow G (1998) *Family Group Conferences in Child Welfare.* Oxford: Blackwells E

Marsh P and Peel M (1999) *Leaving Care in Partnership.* Norwich: The Stationery Office A

Matheson J and Babb P (2000) *Social Trends* 32. London: Office for National Statistics, Stationery Office. Online version available at www.statistics.gov.uk E

Mayfield J, Pennucci A and Lyon C (2002) *Kinship Care in Washington State:*

Prevalence, policy and needs. Washington: Washington State Institute for Public Policy. Online version available at www.wsippa.wa.gov B

Millham S, Bullock R, Hoise K and Hack M (1986) *Lost in Care.* Aldershot: Gower A

Minkler M and Roe K (1993) *Grandmothers As Caregivers.* Newbury Park, CA: Sage B

Modood T, Berthoud R, Lakey J, Nazroo J, Smith P, Virdee S and Beishon S (1997) *Ethnic Minorities in Britian: Disadvantage and diversity.* London: Policy Studies Institute E

Moore R (2000) 'Material Deprivation Amongst Ethnic Minority and White Children: The evidence of the sample of anonymised records' in Bradshaw J and Sainsbury R (eds) *Experiencing Poverty.* Aldershot: Ashgate E

Morgan A (2003) *Survey of Local Authorities in England, Policy and Practice in Family and Friends Care.* London: Family Rights Group A

Morgan R (2006). *About Social Workers: A children's views report.* Newcastle: Office for the Children's Rights Director, Commission for Social Care Inspection E

Morrow V (1998) *Understanding Families: Children's perspectives.* London: National Children's Bureau E

National Foster Care Association (2000) *Family and Friends Carer's Handbook and Family and Friends Carers: Social workers training guide.* London: NFCA G

National Statistics (2005) *Children Looked After by Local Authorities Year Ending 31 March 2004. Volume 1: Commentary and national tables.* Norwich: DfES, Stationery Office E

National Statistics (2006) *Social Services Performance Assessment Framework Indicators, Children 2005-2006.* E

Needell B, Webster D and Barth RP (1996) *Performance Indicators for Child Welfare Services in California.* Berkeley: Child Welfare Research Centre, University of California F

Nixon P (2001) 'Making Kinship Partnerships Work: Examining family group conferences' in Broad B (ed) *Kinship Care: The placement of choice for children and young people.* Lyme Regis: Russell House Publishing G

Nixon P (2007) 'Seen but Not Heard? Children and Young People's Participation in Family Group Decision Making: Concepts and practice issues' *Protecting Children* 22 (1) G

Nixon P, Burford G and Quinn A (with Edelbaum J) (2005) *A Survey of International Practices, Policy and Research on Family Group Conferencing and Related Practices.* Englewood, Colorado: American Humane Association, National Center on Family Group Decision Making B

O'Brien P, Massat CR and Gleeson JP (2001) 'Upping the Ante: Relative caregivers' perceptions of changes in child welfare policies' *Child Welfare* 80 B

O'Brien V (1999) 'Evolving Networks of Relative Care: Some findings from an Irish study' in Greef R (ed) *Fostering Kinship.* Ashgate: Aldershot C

O'Brien V (2000) 'Relative Care: A different type of foster care – implications for practice' in Kelly G and Gilligan R *Issues in Foster Care: Policy, practice and research.* London: Jessica Kingsley G

O'Brien, V. (2001) 'Contributions from an Irish Study: Understanding and managing relative care' in Broad B (ed) *Kinship Care: The placement choice for children and young people.* Lyme Regis: Russell House Publishing C

O'Donnell JM (1999) 'Involvement of African American Fathers in Kinship Foster Care Services' *Social Work* 44 B

O'Donnell JM (2001) 'Paternal Involvement in Kinship Foster Care Services in One Father and Multiple Father Families' *Child Welfare* 80 B

Oppenhiem C and Harper L (1996) *Poverty: The facts*. London: Child Poverty Action Group E

Packman J, Randall J and Jacques N (1986) *Who Needs Care?* Oxford: Blackwell E

Parton N (2001) 'Risk and Professional Judgement' in Cull L and Roche J (eds) *The Law and Social Work: Contemporary issues for practice*. Basingstoke: Open University, Palgrave G

Pecora PJ, Le Prohn NS and Nasuti JJ (1999) 'Role Perceptions of Kinship and Other Foster Parents in Family Foster Care' in Hegar R and Scannapieco M (eds) *Kinship Foster Care: Policy, practice and research*. New York: Oxford University Press F

Pemberton D (1999) 'Fostering in a Minority Community – Travellers in Ireland' in Greef R (ed) *Fostering Kinship*. Aldershot: Ashgate C

Peters J (2005) 'True Ambivalence: Child welfare workers' thoughts, feelings and beliefs about kinship foster care' *Children and Youth Services Review* 27 (6) B

Phillips C (2006) *Kinship Care – Submission Children in Care Green Paper Team*. London: Office of the Children's Commissioner E

Philpot T (2001) *A Very Private Practice. An investigation into private fostering*. London: BAAF Adoption and Fostering A

Pitcher D (2001) 'Assessing Grandparent Carers: A framework' in Broad B (ed) *Kinship Care: The placement choice for children and young people*. Lyme Regis: Russell House Publishing A

Platt L (2007) *Poverty and Ethnicity in the UK*. Bristol: Policy Press, York: Joseph Rowntree Foundation E

Portengen R and van der Neut B (1999) 'Assessing Family Strengths – A family systems approach' in Greeff R (ed) *Fostering Kinship: An international perspective on kinship foster care*. Aldershot: Ashgate C

Preston G (ed) (2005) *At Greatest Risk: The children most likely to be poor*. London: Child Poverty Action Group E

Prior D and Paris A (2005) *Preventing Children's Involvement in Crime – Review of the evidence*. London: Department for Education and Skills E

Pulling J and Summerfield C (eds) (1997) *Social Focus on Families*. London: Office for National Statistics, The Stationery Office E

Quinton D, Rushton A, Dance C and Mayes D (1997) 'Contact Between Children Placed Away from Home and Their Birth Parents: Research issues and evidence' *Clinical Child Psychology and Psychiatry* 2 (3) D

Richards A (2001) *Second Time Around: A survey of grandparents raising their grandchildren*. London: Family Rights Group A

Richards A and Ince L (2000) *Overcoming the Obstacles: Looked after children – quality services for black and minority ethnic children and their families*. London: Family Rights Group E

Richards A and Tapsfield R (2003) *Funding Family and Friends Care: The way forward*. London: Family Rights Group D

Rodning C, Beckwith L, and Howard J (1991) 'Quality of Attachment and Home Environments in Children Prenatally Exposed to PCP Cocaine' *Development and Psychopathology* 3 F

Rowe J, Cain H, Hundleby M and Keane A (1984) *Long Term Foster Care*. London: Batsford A

Rowe J, Hundleby M and Garnett L (1989) *Child Care Now: A survey of child placement patterns*. (Research Series 6) London: BAAF A

Russell C (1995): *Parenting the Second Time Around: Grandparents as carers of young relatives in child protection cases*. (unpublished dissertation) University of East Anglia E

Ryburn M (1995) 'Adopted Children's Identity and Information Needs' *Children and Society* 9 (3) E

Sallnas M, Vinnerlung B and Westermark K (2004) 'Breakdown of Teenage Placements in Swedish Foster and Residential Care' *Child and Family Social Work* 9 (2) C

Sands RG (2000) 'Factors Associated with Stress Among Grandparents Raising their Grandchildren' *Family Relations* 49 (1) B

Sawyer RJ and Dubowitz (1994) 'School Performance of Children in Kinship care' *Child Abuse and Neglect* 18 (7) B

Scannapieco M (1999) 'Kinship Care in the Public Child Welfare System: A systematic review of the research' in Hegar R and Scannapieco M (eds) *Kinship Foster Care: Policy, practice and research*. New York: Oxford University Press F

Scannapieco M and Hegar RL (1999) 'Kinship Foster Care In Context' in Hegar R and Scannapieco M (eds) *Kinship Foster Care: Policy, practice, and research*. New York: Oxford University Press F

Scannapieco M, Hegar R and McAlpine C (1997) 'Kinship Care and Foster Care: A comparison of characteristics and outcomes' *Families in Society: The Journal of Contemporary Human Services* 78 (5) B

Schofield V (2005) 'Third Generation Parenting' *Social Work Now* 30 F

Schwartz AE (2002) 'Societal Value and the Funding of Kinship Care' *The Social Service Review* 76 (3) F

Sheindlin JB (1994) 'Paying Grandparents to Keep Kids in Limbo' (op ed The New York Times, 29 August) cited in McLean B and Thomas TC (1996) 'Informal and Formal Kinship Care Populations: A study in contrasts' *Child Welfare* 75 (5) F

Shlonsky AR and Berrick JD (2001) 'Assessing and Promoting Quality in Kin and Non-kin Foster Care' *Social Service Review* 75 (1) B

Sinclair I (2005) *Fostering Now: Messages from research*. London: Jessica Kingsley D

Sinclair I, Gibbs I and Wilson K (2004) *Foster Placements: Why they succeed and why they fail*. London: Jessica Kingsley E

Sinclair I, Wilson K and Gibbs I (2000) *Supporting Foster Placements. Second report to the Department of Health*. York: Social Work Research and Development Unit, University of York E

Smale G, Tuson G and Stratham D (2000) *Social Work and Social Problems: Working towards social change*. Basingstoke: Macmillan Press G

Smith AB, Gollop MM, Taylor NJ and Atwool NR (1999) *Children in Kinship and Foster Care: Research report*. Dunedin, New Zealand: Children's Issues Centre, University of Otago C

Smith L and Hennessy J (1999) *Making a Difference: Essex family group conference project. Research findings and practice issues*. Chelmsford: Essex County Council

Social Services Department E

Solomon JC and Marx J (1995) 'To Grandmother's House We Go – Health and school adjustment of children raised solely by grandparents' *The Gerontologist* 35 B

Spence N (2004) 'Kinship Care in Australia' *Child Abuse Review* 13 (4) C

Starr RH, Dubowitz H, Harrington D and Feigelman S (1999) 'Behaviour Problems of Teens in Kinship Care' in Hegar R and Scannapieco M (eds) *Kinship Foster Care: Policy, practice and research.* New York: Oxford University Press F

Statistics New Zealand (2002) *New Zealand Official Year Book (2002)* Wellington: Bateman Publishers C

Stelmaszuk ZW (1999) 'The Continuing Role of Kinship Care in a Changing Society' in Greeff R (ed) *Fostering Kinship: An international perspective on kinship foster care.* Aldershot: Ashgate C

Strozier A, Elrod B, Beiler P, Smith A and Carter K (2004) 'Developing a Network of Support for Relative Caregivers' *Children and Youth Services Review* 26 (7) F

Szolnoki J and Cahn K (2002) *African American Kinship Caregivers: Principles for developing supportive programs.* Washinton: University of Washington School of Social Work, Northwest Institute for Children and Families F

Tan S (2000) *Friends and Relative Care: The neglected carers.* (unpublished dissertation for the PQ Award in Social Work) Brunel University A

Terling-Watt T (2001) 'Permanency in Kinship Care: An exploration of disruption rates and factors associated with placement disruption' *Children and Youth Services Review* 23 (2) B

Testa MF (1992) 'Conditions of Risk for Substitute Care' *Children and Youth Services Review* 14 B

Testa MF (1997) 'Kinship Foster Care in Illinois' in Barth RP, Berrick JD and Gilbert N (eds) *Child Welfare Research Review: Volume 2.* New York: Columbia University Press F

Testa M and Rolock N (1999) 'Professional Foster Care: A future worth pursuing?' *Child Welfare* 78 (1) G

Testa MF and Shook-Slack K (2002) 'The Gift of Kinship Foster Care' *Children and Youth Services Review* 24 F

Testa MF, Shook K, Cohen L and Woods M (1999) 'Permanency Planning Options for Children in Formal Kinship Care' *Child Welfare* 75 F

Thoburn J (1996) 'The Research Evidence of the Importance of Links With Relatives When Children Are in Care' in The Grandparents Federation (ed) *The Children Act 1989: What's in it for Grandparents.* Harlow: The Grandparents Federation D

Thoburn J, Lewis A and Shemmings D (1995) Paternalism or Partnership? *Family involvement in the child protection process.* London: HMSO E

Thornton C (1993) *Family Group Conferences: A literature review.* Lower Hutt, New Zealand: Practitioners' Publishing F

Thornton J (1987) *An Investigation into the Nature of the Kinship Foster Home.* (PhD dissertation) New York: Yeshiva University, Wurzweiler School of Social work F

Thornton JL (1991) 'Permanency Planning for Children in Kinship Foster Homes' Child Welfare 70 F

Timmer S, Sedlar G and Urquiza A (2004) 'Challenging Children in Kin Versus Non-kin Foster Care Perceived Costs and Benefits to Caregivers' Child Maltreatment 9 (5) D

Titcomb A and Le Croy C (2005) Outcomes of Arizona's Family Group Decision Making Program, in Protecting Children, Vol 10, No.4, American Humane Association, Colorado F

Trasler G (1960) In Place of Parents. London: Routledge and Kegan Paul E

Trent J (1989) Homeward Bound: The rehabilitation of children to their birth parents. Ilford: Barnardo's E

Tripp De Robertis M and Litrownik AJ (2004) 'The Experience of Foster Care: Relationship between foster parent disciplinary applications and aggression in a sample of young foster children' Child Maltreatment 9 (1) B

Triseliotis J (1980) New Developments in Foster Care and Adoption. London: Routledge and Kegan Paul E

Triseliotis J (1989) 'Foster Care Outcomes: A review of key research findings' Adoption and Fostering 13 D

Triseliotis J, Walker M and Hill M (2000) Delivering Foster Care. London: British Agencies for Adoption and Fostering A

Utting D (1995) Family and Parenthood, Supporting Family Breakdown: A guide to the debate. York: Joseph Rowntree Foundation D

Walton E, Fraser M, Lewis R, Pecora P and Walton W (1993) 'In-home Focussed Reunification: An experimental study' Child Welfare 72 (5) E

Waterhouse S and Brocklesby E (1999) 'Placement Choices for Children: Giving more priority to kinship placements?' in Greeff R (ed) Fostering Kinship. Aldershot: Ashgate D

Webster D, Barth RP and Needell B (2000) 'Placement Stability for Children in Out-of-home Care: A longitudinal analysis' Child Welfare 79 (5) B

Wedge P and Mantle G (1991) Sibling Groups and Social Work: A study of children released for permanent family placement. Aldershot: Avebury E

Weinstein EA (1960) The Self-image of the Foster Child. New York: Russell Sage Foundation F

Wheal A (2001): 'Family and Friends Who Are Carers: A framework for success' in Broad B (ed) Kinship Care: The placement choice for children and young people. Lyme Regis: Russell House Publishing D

Wheal A and Waldman J (1997) Friends and Family as Carers: Identifying the training needs of carers and social workers. London: National Foster Care Association G

Whitley DM, Kelly SJ and Sipe TA (2001) 'Grandmothers Raising Grandchildren: Are they at increased risk of health problems?' Health and Social Work 26 (2) B

Wilson H, Sinclair I, Taylor C, Pithouse A and Sellick C (2004) Fostering Success: An exploration of the research literature on foster care. London: Social Care Institute for Excellence D

Wilson L (1996) The 1995 Annual Client Evaluation. Tulsa, Oklahoma: Wilson Resources B

Woodworth R (1996) 'You're Not Alone ... You're One in a Million' *Child Welfare* 75 (6) F

Wulczyn F and George R (1992) 'Foster Care in New York and Illinois: The challenge of rapid change' *Social Service Review* 66 (2) F

Yorker BC, Kelley SJ, Whitney D, Lewis A, Magis J, Bergeron A and Napier C (1998) 'Custodial Relationships of Grandparents Raising Grandchildren: Results of a home-based intervention study' *Juvenile and Family Court Journal* 49 (2) F

Young M and Willmott P (1962) *Family and Kinship in East London*. London: Pelican A

Zimmerman E, Daykin D, Moore V, Wuu C and Li J (1998) *Kinship and Non-kinship Foster Care in New York City: Pathways and outcomes*. New York: United Way of New York City F

Zuravin S, Benedict M and Somerfield M (1997) 'Child Maltreatment in Family Foster Care: Foster home correlates' in Barth RP, Berrick JD and Gilbert N (eds) *Child Welfare Research Review: Volume 2*. New York: Columbia University Press F

index

about the author

Paul Nixon is a social worker and Assistant Director (Children's Social Care) for the Children and Young People's Service, North Yorkshire. He has worked for the last 17 years in Local Authorities with children, young people and their families.

Paul's main interests are safeguarding children, family support, kinship placement and child, family and community participation. He has organised a number of international conferences on Family Group Conferences and provided training and consultancy both around the UK and abroad. He has published numerous articles and chapters and is co-author of 'Empowering Practice? A critical appraisal of the Family Group Conference approach' (1999 Policy Press) and 'Children growing up with relatives and friends' (2004 Family Rights Group). He is currently editing a book on Family Group Conferences for the Family Rights Group.

about **research** in **practice**

research in **practice** is a department of The Dartington Hall Trust run in collaboration with the University of Sheffield, the Association of Directors of Children's Services and our network of over 100 participating agencies in England and Wales.

Our mission is to promote positive outcomes for children and families through proper and greater use of research evidence. Our services are designed to improve access to research and strengthen its understanding and adoption through the promotion of evidence-informed practice.

More information is available on our website: **www.rip.org.uk** where you can also subscribe to:

- our monthly *What's New* email
- our quarterly newsletter *NetWork*.

research in **practice** publications can be purchased from the website **www.rip.org.uk/publications** or by contacting our Dartington Office: Blacklers, Park Road, Dartington, Totnes, Devon, TQ9 6EQ
t: 01803 867692 f: 01803 868816 e: ask@rip.org.uk

contributing to a sustainable future for children and families

research in **practice** aims to improve outcomes for vulnerable children and families in England and Wales by promoting and facilitating evidence-informed practice. To recognise our role as members of the wider global community, we will donate 25% of the sale of this book and our other publications to a designated international charitable project to support a sustainable future for children and families in need. Details of the project identified for support each year are on our website:
www.rip.org.uk/charity

This paper is produced with 100% Elemental Chlorine Free pulp and is fully recyclable. It is manufactured from50% post-consumer recycled fibre.

research in practice is a department of The Dartington Hall Trust, registered in England as a company limited by guarantee and a charity www.dartington.org
The Dartington Hall Trust is a registered charity no. 279756; Company no. 1485560; VAT no. 402196875
Registered Office: The Elmhirst Centre, Dartington Hall, Totnes, Devon TQ9 6EL